The
Hair-Raising
Joys of
Raising
Boys

Books by

Dave Meurer

Daze of Our Wives
If You Want Breakfast in Bed, Sleep in the Kitchen
Good Spousekeeping
You Can Childproof Your Home, but They'll Still Get In

The Hair-Raising Joys of Raising Boys

DAVE MEURER

SPIRE

Published by Fleming H. Revell
a division of Baker Publishing Group
P.O. Box 6287, Grand Rapids, MI 49516-6287
www.revellbooks.com

Spire edition published 2006
ISBN 10: 0-8007-8729-3
ISBN 978-0-8007-8729-5

Fourth printing, September 2006

Previously published under the title *Boyhood Daze* by Bethany House
Publishers.

Printed in the United States of America.

To Dale,

my wonderful partner in life,
who has always believed in me and
whose love made this book
(not to mention our kids)
possible.

And to Mark and Brad,

the two *great* boys
God has privileged us to raise,
both of whom are nevertheless
still *grounded* for making fun
of my bald spot.
That will teach you!

DAVE MEURER works for the United States House of Representatives as an aide to a California congressman. He is the winner of numerous state and national writing awards and honors. His writings have appeared in major publications, including *Focus on the Family* and *Homelife*. The Meurer family lives in northern California.

Dave Meurer can be reached at www.davemeurer.com.

Acknowledgments

The poet tells us that "No man is an island." Well, no man is a Volkswagen either, for that matter. But the poetic point here is that we are all connected to others, and those others help us succeed in life.

The one who has helped me the most is my wife, the love of my life, Dale. This book would not have happened without her encouragement and support. Of the myriad blessings in my life, she is the greatest. Dale, thanks for saving up the money to send me to the Mount Hermon Christian Writers Conference, and then insisting that I go. Oh, thanks for going through all that pregnancy and labor stuff, too. The book would have been a bit skimpy without your involvement.

I also owe a huge debt of gratitude to our two boys, Mark and Brad, who allowed me to share so much about their lives, trials, and tribulations, and only insisted on 25 percent of the net profits (each). All kidding aside, they are a tremendous joy as well as a never-ending source of book material. Thanks, guys!

A big hug and kiss go to my parents, Bob and Doris Meurer. They loved me, brought books into my life, and encouraged my writing from my very earliest days in grade school. They have also been relentless cheerleaders throughout the process of completing this project. Thanks, Mom and Dad!

A bulging, industrial-sized canister of thanks goes to Steve Laube, my illustrious editor, who, upon reading the first chapter, broke into convulsions of unbridled mirth and immediately persuaded Bethany House Publishers to take a chance on this new author. Steve, thanks for all the e-mails, laughter, and encouragement. (Does your boss know you are snickering on company time?)

Four cubic yards of gratitude also goes to Kevin Johnson, Jeanne Mikkelson, Lance Wubbels, and Kris "The Cheez Whiz" Landis for assorted assistance ranging from *extremely* last-minute changes in the cover design, to great publicity, to putting up with bothersome pestering from me when they had *lots* of other stuff to do.

I hurl a heaping shovelful of thanks at Tim Holler, my best friend for more than two decades, who not only reviewed (and laughed at) my manuscript, but who has been a stable source of support and inspiration for years. Tim, Pam, kids—dinner at Corky's is on me.

Finally, and quite seriously, I am deeply grateful to God, with whom nothing is impossible.

Contents

Prologue

Please skip the prologue and go directly to chapter 1.

I have never understood why authors even write prologues, because most readers simply ignore them. I know I do.

I think that anything important should appear in the body of the book, not be tucked away in some obscure paragraph that most people will skip. The only reason I am even including a prologue is that everybody expects to find one. I am afraid that if I don't provide something to disregard, then roughly 80 percent of readers will skip chapter 1 by accident.

If you are still reading by now, you clearly have the same problem my boys have in following directions. The VERY FIRST sentence in the prologue explicitly said to skip this section and go to chapter 1. Was there something terribly unclear about that? Do you have any idea how difficult it is to get my boys to follow extremely simple instructions only to have adults, such as yourself, providing such a poor example?

What are you going to do next, spray graffiti on the next-door neighbor's poodle? Just what kind of role model are you? How do you hope to successfully raise boys when you, personally, cannot even obey a simple directive?

Fortunately for you, help is as close as chapter 1.

Cordially,
Dave Meurer

Chapter 1

Infant Male Weaponry

—or—

Surviving the Ballistic Diaper

I note with great interest that when God made the first human being, Adam, He created him as a complete adult and thus totally bypassed diapers, colic, toddlerhood, adolescence, and driving lessons.

Hey, if I were all-powerful I would have done the same thing. So this observation is certainly not a criticism.

My personal theory is that God designed parenthood, in part, as an enormous character-building exercise, and since God does not personally require character improvement, He didn't need to bother getting Adam to eat strained peas.

But part of our lot in life as imperfect humans is that wedded bliss holds a high degree of likelihood that one of you is going to get pregnant, and when you do, there is a 50-50 chance in each and every pregnancy that you will end up with a baby boy, which means you will also end up facing all of the interesting things that baby boys do.

NOTE: I am not going to spend a great deal of time

on the *having* of babies, as this is a book on boy raising, not boy birthing. Suffice it to say, however, that
there are a variety of classes in virtually every com-
munity in America that will explain various methods
to prepare for as calm and pain-free a delivery as possible, and they are all run by the same people who create those television ads for the Marine Corps that
make boot camp actually look like a frolic at the
county fair (albeit a fair in which everyone is heavily
armed).

What a bunch of pranksters.
I did *exactly* what they said to do, even the
breathing exercises, and nevertheless the real birth was
nothing like the practice run. In the class, none of the
women were sweating like prizefighters in the ninth
round. And they didn't scream at people, either. But
once we were in the labor room, every time I tried to
offer my wife helpful advice like "Try to pretend it
doesn't hurt so much" and "Try not to dig your finger-
nails so deeply into the bed frame," she replied with
sharply unappreciative comments.

So I am going to skip this harrowing initial phase
of the parenthood process, other than to note that as
long as they get a baby out of the deal, women tend
to be very forgiving after the first couple of days.

But I digress.

This chapter is actually about baby boy warfare.

Although your baby boy comes camouflaged as an
almost unbelievably darling little cherub, complete
with gurgling little coos and murmurs that will absolutely captivate your heart, he nevertheless comes into
this world heavily armed to do battle with you, the

trusting and unsuspecting parent.

This should not be all that surprising when you think about it. In the natural world, there are many plants that pack such a toxic punch they can actually kill you within hours if you ingest them. (I am NOT talking here about spinach or zucchini, which only *appear* to result in the throes of death when you serve them to boys, even if they never so much as swallow a molecule, which, trust me, they won't.)

If many everyday garden flowers come so heavily armed, it should not be terribly surprising that apparently harmless baby boys also have a significant offensive capability, which I shall now outline for you. Keep this list posted in a handy place.

The Baby Boy Weapons Arsenal

1. The Ballistic Warhead Diaper. This is a full-fledged, maximum-power detonation and includes spectacular sound effects. He will typically launch this one in a crowded public area to inflict the greatest number of casualties. Be particularly alert when you are out to dinner with friends. He can clear an entire restaurant in moments.

2. The Stealth Diaper. This is one of the more deadly weapons in your baby's arsenal. The ordnance is delivered quietly, with no telltale grimacing or fussing. You have no clue there is any danger until it is too late and you have picked him up to do that little trick where you hold him above your head and wiggle him and suddenly your shirt is history. (One enterprising dad I know mailed his ruined sweat shirt to the

National Endowment for the Arts, and they gave him a federal grant for his "grim yet captivating statement about the excesses of capitalism"—thus offering tangible proof that parenthood has its rewards.)

3. The Cruise Diaper. A terrain-hugging device, utilized by toddlers, that requires an advanced level of agility that cannot be attained by crawlers. The Cruise Diaper can last several giggling chases around the lawn and is carefully timed to explode when Dad suddenly goes for the playful tackle. It is outlawed by the Geneva Convention, which means nothing to your toddler because he can't read.

4. The Underwater Mine. If you saw *The Hunt for Red October*, trust me, this is worse than anything the Russians ever deployed at sea. I have seen adults launch themselves, missile-like, right out of the deep end of a pool and onto dry land when one of these weapons is detonated. The secret to safely taking your baby boy into water is to ensure you are using someone else's pool.

5. The Intercontinental Ballistic Diaper. This is *by far* the most lethal of all diapers. It is used exclusively on civilian airline flights between the U.S. and distant nations and is only detonated when the aircraft is out over the ocean and thus cannot make an emergency landing unless the pilot is willing to ditch into shark-infested waters. Many times, this option is worth taking. Bear in mind that modern jets have a completely sealed environment and you just keep breathing the same recycled air over and over and over again. When planning your trip to Australia, you should therefore carefully consider taking the USS *Nimitz,* even though it means you have to join the navy for four years.

But even though you are completely forewarned about the fragrance-related dangers associated with your baby boy, the harsh fact remains that you, as a parent, are going to be called upon to rescue your child from some truly awful diapers. There is no escaping this. God arranged it this way for reasons we can only speculate about.

Think it over. Of all the creatures God created, we are the only ones that have to deal with diapers. Consider the lilies of the field; they neither toil nor spin nor clean up after their junior lily offspring. Consider the birds of the air; the parent birds simply teach the fledglings to aim for your freshly washed car and then they go back to the nest and make humorous little chirps about it.

And then there is that large and mysterious sea creature the Bible refers to as the Leviathan. Whatever it is, you can bet it does not clean up after all the little Leviathans, even though this means that, essentially, it lives in an enormous commode (and that without the benefit of Tidy Bowl).

So why did God saddle us humans with this particularly nasty task? It isn't as though we HAD to come equipped with—not one, but TWO—intestines. I mean, look at your hydrangeas. They get to take in carbon dioxide and give off oxygen. No muss, no fuss, and certainly no squeezing the Charmin. (This also *really* cuts down on their grocery expenses.)

You cannot convince me that an omnipotent God couldn't have designed us with different plumbing.

After all, angels don't have to take potty breaks.

No, we are left with the inescapable fact that, although He could have planned otherwise, God deliberately chose to create our babies as hygienically challenged little people who require our extremely personal service several times each day.

So again we have to ask, "Why?"

I go back to my hypothesis, outlined at the beginning of this chapter, that God has created parenthood as a massive character-building exercise. He tells us to love our children, care for them, protect them, and, if necessary, lay down our lives for them. After all, that is what Jesus did by His example.

I think one reason God created babies the way He did is to ensure that we learn to perform a selfless act on behalf of a truly helpless person who cannot even thank us, doesn't really know what we are doing for him anyway, and, more likely than not, will pee on us for good measure.

There are no awards for changing the baby. No Congressional Medals of Honor. No acclaim in the *New York Times*—"Man Rescues Infant From Hideous Diaper of Doom!"

Changing the baby is sort of like giving alms in secret, only smellier.

I remember the first time I was stranded at home *completely* alone with Mark. Up to that point, I had weaseled out of most of the truly awful diapers. Between Dale, my wife, and two doting grandmothers (who almost seemed to *enjoy* changing diapers), I was able to avoid the most serious diaper events.

I had a wild hope that this would continue until Mark was potty trained. But Dale was gone, and Mark had just emitted what could very well earn him an entry in the *Guinness Book of World Records* for the Most Horrific Diaper in the History of the Western Hemisphere.

I cannot even begin to describe how awful this was. Paint was literally peeling off the walls before my eyes. FEMA ordered an emergency evacuation of a four-county area. The dog was lunging wildly for the door, *and it was a stuffed animal.*

I prayed for Dale to come home suddenly as I placed Mark on the changing pad.

(You female readers, if you have stuck with me this far, are probably saying, "What a sniveling little WIMP! Just CHANGE THE BABY! How DARE you wait around for your poor wife to come home and bail you out, you little COWARD!!! Why are you making such a BIG DEAL out of a stupid DIAPER anyway? It isn't like you are going off to BATTLE!!")

Hey, I would have GLADLY taken on an entire tank division armed with nothing more than a box of scented wipes if someone would have given me the choice. Not meaning to sound retrograde or sexist or anything, but women have a much easier time with diapers because of the Mom Gene. Scientists* have conclusively proved that females have an interesting quirk in their DNA that renders them much more able than men to tidy up after the baby.

It isn't our fault that we were born with the Dad Gene, which allows us to shoot, gut, and dress out an elk in half the time it takes us to change a messy dia-

---

*OK, they were all *guy* scientists who had infants at home. But that does not necessarily mean they were not objective.

per. God made us this way. I think we should be commended for even *attempting* to change the baby without the superior advantage of the Mom Gene. While I'm on the subject of the Dad Gene, I should also point out that this particular genetic trait is also responsible for our tendency to buy power tools we don't need and will likely never use, so please just lighten up on us.

But back to the diaper crisis.

I got Mark as ready as I possibly could without actually changing him.

I had the Fresh Scent Wipes ready.

I had a warm, soapy washcloth.

I had a new diaper ready to go.

I had a bucket of Lysol.

I was ready to grit my teeth, plunge in, and do what I had to do, which was supposed to be God's cue that, inasmuch as I had proven my willingness to make this huge sacrifice, He could intervene and send an angel to actually do the heavy lifting.

But there was no blinding flash of light. No heavenly assistance. No knock at the door.

Just me and my son.

As I faced Mark, I was suddenly filled with shame at my hesitation and also a grim determination to save him from that vile diaper *right now*. He was *my kid* and I loved him too much to leave him in that mess. So I gagged and wheezed and perspired through an ordeal that only God and I really understood.

I not only changed Mark, but I myself was changed in that process. This may sound ridiculously melodramatic, but it is true. I mean, we are talking about the most awful diaper in recorded history being changed by the guy who set the American Medical Association's National Standard for the Gag Reflex. In a small way, I died to myself that day. I did something that I honestly thought I could not do. And I did it because I loved Mark more than I loved myself.

In a strange way, it was a magic moment. I was worn out, but pleased I had rescued him. He was cooing and being all cute and feeling much better as I let him "air out." I felt a tangible warmth spreading across my chest.

It was pee.

Chapter 2

Boy, Are YOU in for It!

Have you ever noticed that bestselling books on raising male children invariably have titles which hint, almost charmingly, that you are in for a challenging task, but never come right out and say that you are, in fact, doomed?

They are titled *The Challenge of Boys*, or *Raising the Male Child: the Joys and the Struggles*, or *Your Boys— More Than Just Primitive Carbon-Based Life-Forms*.

Authors do this because careful market research indicates that parents are *much* more likely to purchase a book that offers hope and reassurance than a book that tells you, point-blank, that raising boys is a monumental, multiyear battle to simply get them to eat zucchini, not to mention mold them into mature and responsible Christian young men.

Very few authors will attempt to sell you a book titled *Raising Boys—Face It, You're Doomed!* But because I accept the biblical prohibition against deceiving others, that is exactly what I titled this book until my uptight editor demanded a more chipper, upbeat title.

But once you accept the original premise of this

book—namely, you're doomed—you can get down to the practical matter of actually doing the job.

Now, what do we mean by "you're doomed"? We mean, right off the bat, that you should notice we are speaking of ourselves in the third person. This is usually a prerogative of the queen of England but also occurs in the speech patterns of the mentally disturbed. It means that we are either batty or are raising boys, unless this book is being penned by Her Majesty.

But I digress.

You'll digress quite a bit too if you raise boys.

You will be tucking one of them into bed, for example, and talking to him about his class field trip to the museum tomorrow when you suddenly discover that this kid's face is *absolutely filthy and he just finished his bath twenty minutes ago*! And you'll ask what in the WORLD did he do between the bathroom and his bedroom, and he will reply, "Nothing!" which is what they ALWAYS say, and you will finally discover that he has a package of Jell-O Dutch Chocolate Pudding Mix under his pillow and he has been eating the powder with his hands and now you have to wash all the sheets and he needs another bath because he is a boy and you are doomed. Get used to it.

When I say that you are doomed, I do not at all mean to imply that your boy has a high propensity to become a dropout or a felon or a senior White House advisor. In fact, you will notice that I have never even hinted that your boy will be anything other than a good and noble young man who will marry a very wonderful woman and have a challenging and productive career and teach Sunday school and give you wonderful grandchildren. I never said your kid is doomed. I said *you* are.

Let me clarify for you exactly what I mean.

For starters, virtually everything you do, no matter how well intentioned or innocent it seems at the time, will eventually be twisted and mutated by your boys to embarrass you until the end of the world.

EXAMPLE: When our children were toddlers, my wife, Dale, and I made a deliberate decision to use non-offensive euphemisms for various bodily functions so that our children would not suddenly leap up during church and shout, "I have to PEE RIGHT NOW!"

Our euphemism for flatulence, or "gas," was "fluff." One would not think this could become a constant source of embarrassment and irritation. But one would only think that if one did not have boys in the home.

When our old clothes dryer finally gave up the ghost one year, we replaced it with a new unit that included a handy feature designed to periodically tumble the clothes until you removed them, thus cutting down on wrinkles. We purchased this dryer when Mark was eight and Bradley was six.

This handy cycle is called the "fluff setting."

Every single time we have done laundry since then, the following joke is told by one of our boys: "Hey, I hope you remembered to FLUFF the clothes!!!! HA! HA! HA! HA! HA! HA!"

We HATE this joke. This is not even REMOTELY funny! This is an incredibly dumb, infantile, tacky remark. So, of course, we are DOOMED to hear it again and again and again until our seventy-fifth wedding anniversary.

But why are boys this way? They certainly don't pick it up from us! Dale and I don't run around the house making bad puns about flatulence and placing live amphibians in our pockets and sneaking them into our sock drawers (more on this in my upcoming book titled *Don't Open Their Sock Drawers Unless You X-Ray the Contents, Especially if You Hear Scratching Sounds*). Nor does the typical mom fling herself down on the supermarket floor and have a shrieking fit in an attempt to get someone to buy her a chocolate bar (unless she is having a *very* bad day, in which case you'd better just get it for her).

Little boys (and big ones as well), on the other hand, are capable of all kinds of awful and selfish behavior. So again, we must ask, "Why?"

Theologians will tell you that the core problem with humans is that we are born with what is known as a "sin nature." That is, children, as wonderful and innocent as they seem at birth, have a predisposition to be pugnacious, selfish, and dishonest, and only a spiritual conversion and the constant moral guidance and discipline of responsible adults will keep children on the straight and narrow path—particularly if they are wearing roller blades.

Left to themselves, children will grow up to be self-indulgent barbarians. (A few modern celebrities come to mind.)

As grim and scary as this may sound, we can be encouraged, because the Bible is chock-full of instruction regarding how we can raise our boys to be noble, compassionate, faithful leaders of the next generation. While parenting is never an easy task, there is an enormous amount of wisdom and insight found in the pages of the Scriptures. We will explore many of these insights in future chapters.

Regrettably, the Bible is rather silent on the issue of belching.

It is our boys' obsession with belching that really drives Dale and me up the wall.

PARENTING TIP: Never let your boys have a carbonated beverage. Ever.

They will soon discover that by gulping down a soda and deliberately swallowing extra air, they can emit a sustained burp that can exceed twenty-five seconds. And they will do this relentlessly until they begin dating. They will do this during meals, in Sunday school, during a tour of the Sistine Chapel, or in the middle of an historic address by the Surgeon General to a Joint Session of Congress—an event to which you have been invited because you discovered a cure for cancer and you are being honored during a nationally broadcast ceremony.

Surgeon General: "And in recognition of your service to humanity . . ."

NBC anchorman (whispering): "It is a solemn moment indeed as the Surgeon General prepares to . . ."

Your son: "BUUUUUURRRRRRRRRRRRRRRP!"

Boys have no shame.
But you sure will.

Chapter 3

The Moral Training of Boys

—or—

The Eyes of Texas Are Upon You

The moral training of your boys is of paramount importance. If each generation does not pass on basic standards of right and wrong, and cultivate in its children the ability to resist what is bad and choose what is good, we face the very real prospect of our kids becoming little barbarians and getting into trouble with the law and having unstable relationships and eventually getting jobs as congressional aides.

The moral training of your boys is so critical that you should never try it yourself unless you are Billy Graham.

I tried moral training one day when Mark and Brad were quite young, and after a very close call I decided to leave it to the professionals. If I can't even tune up my lawn mower, what makes me think I can impart character to the same children who cackle hysterically and roll on the living room floor every time an advertisement comes on for Preparation H?

As a rank amateur, one day I called the family

together and opened the Bible to the story of David and Goliath. My intent was to demonstrate, at this impressionable age, that if we trust in God and stand for what is good and right, it is possible to overcome obstacles that are far bigger than ourselves.

What actually occurred, however, fell short of the lesson goal.

I had scarcely begun to outline the drama of the fateful battle when Bradley, then four, immediately wanted to know if our commode would possibly suffice if Goliath felt a need to use it. I had rather deftly sidestepped that unpleasant question by noting that all the giants were now dead, so we really don't have to confront that dilemma. It certainly isn't anything addressed by Miss Manners.

But Bradley merely shifted to another, almost identically unpleasant inquiry.

"Since Goliath was a giant, if he sneezed would his booger be the size of a golf ball?"

My other son, who is two years older and far more theologically astute, argued that it would be more the size of a pizza. That reply created a furious debate over what size of pizza it would be: small, medium, or large. It also reminded them that they were hungry, and could we please, please, please go to the pizza parlor?

We have still not finished the story of David and Goliath. Their Sunday school teacher said he would do it for twenty bucks.

One of the problems with imparting moral guidance to young boys is that they fidget or completely ignore you or simply fail to get the point of the lesson when you are doing everything in your power to teach them, and then they turn around and pay obsessive amounts of attention when you don't mean for them to do so.

For example, Mark and I were driving to the store one day (when he was about five) when we pulled up behind another car at a stoplight. When the light changed, the elderly woman driver just sat there as though she were waiting for a more pleasant shade of emerald to come along.

"It's not going to get any greener, lady," I muttered under my breath.

"I don't think she heard you," Mark said.

"That's OK," I replied.

"Maybe if you rolled the window down and yelled it real loud she would hear you," he continued.

"I didn't really want her to hear me, buddy," I explained, perspiration breaking out on my upper lip.

Mark cast a quizzical look my direction.

"Then why did you say it?" he asked.

"I was just kind of mad that she was waiting when the light changed," I admitted.

"Mom says that if you can't say something nice, don't say anything at all."

"Sorry, Mark."

"That's OK," he said. "Just remember for next time."

See what I mean? You can waste hours and hours trying to get them to pay attention to valuable moral lessons, to no avail, and then they just pick some little personal flaw you have, such as berating other drivers behind their backs, and turn it into some big deal! Boys have an incredible problem with focusing on the issue at hand.

And it gets worse. A few years ago, Mark was in the boys' rest room at school and found some money lying on a counter. Do you know what he did? *He took it directly to the school office and gave it to the principal!* Not only did the principal nearly have a stroke, but to add insult to injury we had never even had a moral lesson on this! He certainly didn't pick this up from our fiasco with David and Goliath! This is incredibly frustrating.

Giving back money that you find lying around is something that I had planned to work up to through a methodical series of moral training sessions. The concept should have been clearly over his head, and he completely blew my training schedule.

As it turns out, he picked this concept up YEARS ahead of schedule when he saw me return $100 to a camera store after I discovered they had incorrectly rung up a sale and shorted themselves by that amount. So we clearly see that the inability of boys to appropriately benefit from planned moral training sessions means they are often going to pick up their moral training on a completely unpredictable, willy-nilly basis as they do stuff with you.

This means you have to REALLY be on your toes, because they are watching you like some super-secret Russian spy satellite.

Don't you find this *unnerving*?

Where is Billy Graham when you need him?

Chapter 4

Outsmarting Your Boys
(Don't Even Try It)

In the course of listening to my two boys as they played together, I was struck by how readily my youngest son took instructions from his brother.

"Let's put the train tracks together now," said Mark, the kindergartner, to Bradley, his three-year-old sibling.

"OK!" replied Bradley excitedly.

Now, these are the same two dwarves who, fifteen minutes earlier, had reacted to *my* suggestion that they set up the train tracks as though I had sentenced them to twenty years of eating eggplant.

In a blinding flash of comprehension, it occurred to me that if I could learn to tap into that spirit of brotherly cooperation, I could significantly ease the task of parenting. Why, I could be just like Tom Sawyer, who made his peers eager to whitewash the fence while he relaxed in the shade and chuckled. I could get my boys to work for me instead of against me and they would think it was fun to boot!

Elated with my hypothesis, I decided to test it

immediately. Bradley had earlier in the day been diagnosed with an ear infection and I had not yet attempted to give him his medicine (for much the same reason that I hesitate to force-feed an enraged polar bear).

Getting liquefied antibiotic down the throat of a preschooler, even if it is cleverly colored and scented like a cheap strawberry milk shake, takes endurance that no marathon runner ever dreamed possible. It is, at the absolute minimum, a hard-fought, twenty-minute battle.

"Mark," I whispered, motioning him to come closer, "Bradley has a yucky ear infection and the doctor said he needs to take some medicine to get better. Would you help me explain to him that he needs to do what the doctor says?"

Mark grinned widely and nodded, clearly thrilled with his crucial task.

I glanced at the kitchen clock so that I could accurately record, for the scientific record, the time saved by utilizing my experimental method.

"Bradley," I announced, "Mark has something important to tell you and you must listen closely."

Mark wiped the smile off his face, turned to Bradley, and announced with the grave tone of a concerned surgeon, "Bradley, if you don't take your medicine you are going to die in two hours."

Bradley gasped.

I gasped.

Mark turned to me with a triumphant smile.

"That's not what I said!" I blurted out.

"Is I'm going to heaven?" Bradley asked.

"No, no, no!" I spluttered.

"We are too going to heaven because Jesus loves us," Mark shot back, glaring at me.

"But not right now!" I bellowed as Bradley's eyes filled with tears.

"I only want to go if I get to be in a airplane," insisted Bradley.

"You can't go to heaven in a airplane because it takes too long," Mark corrected with theological precision.

"Well, then I'm not going to go," Bradley replied defiantly.

"You have to because the doctor said," Mark continued helpfully.

"The doctor did not say that!" I retorted.

"Well," Bradley said, ignoring my every word, "let's just lock the doctor up in jail."

"You have to pay lots of money to the policeman to lock up the naughty doctors," Mark explained patiently.

"Let's get our banks!" replied Bradley.

"LISTEN TO ME!" I roared as they scampered down the hall to raid their life savings. "The doctor is **not** naughty and you are **not** going to put him in jail and Bradley is **not** going to die and he just needs to take his medicine!"

I was drowned out by the sounds of loose change cascading to the floor.

I took a moment to calm myself by quickly removing several handfuls of excess hair, then I stomped down the hall to Bradley's room.

"Now listen," I began but was immediately interrupted by Mark.

"How much does a Baskin Robbins ice-cream

cone cost?" he inquired, clutching a handful of his college fund.

"Yeah, how much quarters?" chimed in Bradley.

"Uh, well, uh, about four quarters," I stammered, thrown off track by the speed with which they had shifted gears.

"Yea! We get to have a Baskin Robbins ice-cream cone," they shrieked in delighted unison.

"I didn't say that!" I retorted.

But I knew I was in trouble. In the bizarre logic of children, merely acquiescing to discuss Baskin Robbins is the same as signing in blood that you are going to straightaway indulge in a minimum of two of the thirty-one flavors.

"Look," I said apologetically but firmly. "We can't have ice cream. The doctor said that Bradley can't have anything made out of milk until his ear infection is gone or it will just get worse. Ice cream is made out of milk."

Bradley burst into tears.

But I was pleasantly astonished to watch Mark reach over and give him a comforting hug. I didn't know he was capable of that kind of sympathy in the face of such a monumental disappointment. And I was proud that our parenting labors were producing such mature and selfless behavior in our offspring.

"It's OK, Bradley," said Mark soothingly. "Me and Dad will just go by ourselves and you can wait here with Mom."

"No one is having ice cream!" I snapped.

Then it was stereophonic tears.

"I'll tell you what," I said as the torrent rose above

my knees, "we can still do something fun, even though we can't have ice cream."

"What?" asked Bradley warily.

"Um, popcorn! How about popcorn?" I replied, shooting a warning glance at Mark lest he fill Bradley's head with competing alternatives.

"You have to have a movie or else popcorn isn't fun," Mark managed to point out, which was no small feat considering that I had my hand clamped firmly over his mouth.

Three hours later, after a trip to the video store, two batches of popcorn, and the action-packed adventures of Davy Crockett, Bradley finally swallowed his medicine.

A net loss of two hours and forty minutes. So much for the theory of harnessing brotherly cooperation to improve parental efficiency.

PARENTING TIP: When facing the task of getting your son to swallow his medicine, you should first set the medicine out on the kitchen counter, then, in a firm voice, call your son into the room and hand him over to the lion trainer you have hired for the occasion.

HELPFUL REMINDER: You're doomed.

Chapter 5

Cherished Family Traditions and Other Dangers

Routines are extremely important to your boys, particularly when they are younger. Totally unbeknownst to you, from their earliest days you, the parent, are establishing patterns and key events that will provide an important sense of order and predictability for your impressionable little guys. Many of these routines will become their treasured traditions and will haunt you for the rest of your born days.

I'm not talking here about obvious routines like feeding times and naps and brutal fights with the pediatrician. I'm talking about things that become so important to your boys that they border on the obsessive and you can never stop doing them without risking severe psychological damage and the real possibility that your children will become kleptomaniacs and end up being quoted in the newspaper blaming YOU when they are arrested for trying to steal the hubcaps off the presidential limousine because when they were four years old YOU stopped doing THE ROUTINE.

What is even more scary is that you only have to do something *once* for it to become firmly established in your son's mind as a tradition rivaling the Macy's Thanksgiving Day Parade. Dale and I learned this the hard way when Mark was almost three. We had just picked up our Christmas tree and were driving home when Mark asked where the "little things with the holes that you eat" were.

Dale and I exchanged a quizzical glance. Then Dale remembered that the prior Christmas we had, in fact, bought donuts at the same time we picked up our tree. Bear in mind that Mark was only about twenty months old at that time. We were astonished that he could remember such a seemingly insignificant event.

But from the perspective of a two-year-old, having someone give you a donut is a REALLY BIG DEAL on a par with someone handing you the Crown Jewels of Denmark. It makes an impression.

So we turned the car around and picked up a dozen assorted donuts and have feasted on donuts every year since then while we decorate our tree.

"What a charming and unique tradition," you might say, especially if you have the analytical skills of a toad.

Sure, it worked out OK *that* time. But what if, instead of donuts, we happened to stop and pick up a new toilet plunger? We would have enough plungers to open Dave 'n' Dale's Toilet Emporium by the time the kids are in college.

Or what if we had picked up a box of Sugar Jets cereal, which *they don't make anymore*? Would you want to risk dashing your son's fondest Yuletide tradition on the jagged rocks of a cruel marketing decision by General Mills, Inc.?

So we see that ANYTHING can become an important tradition to your sons at ANY time and YOU WON'T KNOW ABOUT IT UNTIL IT IS TOO LATE, and it ONLY HAS TO HAPPEN ONCE, so the moral of this story is that you should NEVER DO ANYTHING that you are not willing to risk having become a CRITICALLY IMPORTANT LIFE EXPERIENCE that you will have to repeat AGAIN AND AGAIN AND AGAIN until you *DIE.*

This fact was powerfully brought home to me when Mark and Brad were in kindergarten and pre-school (respectively) and I read them *The Cat in the Hat* one fateful evening before tucking them into bed.

They LOVED this story.

They ADORED this story.

They wanted this story the next night.

And the next.

And the next.

And the next.

And the next.

And you can see a trend developing here.

We read this story EVERY SINGLE NIGHT FOR TWO SOLID MONTHS UNTIL I WAS CERTI-FIED BY OUR FAMILY DOCTOR AS MENTALLY DERANGED.

I finally couldn't take it anymore.

"Guys, I have a great idea!" I said as I tucked them into bed. "I'm going to give you a brand-new story tonight!"

"We want *The Cat in the Hat*," they replied in unison.

"But this is a VERY SPECIAL story," I replied, trying to sound enthusiastic as adrenaline coursed through my veins.

"We want *The Cat in the Hat.*"

"Just listen to my idea. . . ."

"We want *The Cat in the Hat.*"

The negotiations were reminiscent of the arduous talks former Secretary of State Henry Kissinger used to conduct with the Soviet Minister of the Bureau of Not Budging an Inch.

We finally compromised on a plan in which I would tell them a new story and *also* read them *The Cat in the Hat* if they didn't like my new tale.

PARENTING TIP: Your boys will immediately take you up on any suggestion that has the net result of extending their bedtime, even if it means late-night dental surgery.

So now I had my big chance.

The boys were sporting broad grins, eyes sparkling, little hands clutching the covers as they waited for me to FAIL so they could cackle hysterically while I was forced to read *The Cat in the Hat* yet one more time.

"I need your help with this story, guys," I began, keenly aware that the last shred of my sanity hung on my ability to capture their imagination and support.

"You each think up something you want in a story, and I'll make up a story about your subjects."

"A submarine!" shouted Mark.

"Cheese!" squealed Brad.

I have a friend in the army who once told me that standard procedure once you realize you are in an ambush is to launch a frontal assault on the enemy because standing still simply guarantees you will be shot to pieces. This had all the hallmarks of a setup, but I plunged desperately ahead.

"Once upon a time," I began, and launched into an exciting and incredibly stupid story about a group of mice who thought that a big chunk of Swiss cheese was actually their apartment complex. They couldn't understand why it kept getting smaller and smaller (it was being slowly sliced up in a delicatessen), and they finally had to leave in search of a new home.

The mice found an old plastic milk carton and, for reasons that sound perfectly rational when you are not yet in first grade, turned it into a submarine and launched it at the city pool and had a lot of exciting adventures, which I am too embarrassed to repeat, and then it was bedtime.

They LOVED this story.

They ADORED this story.

They wanted this story the next night.

Hey, anything was better than *The Cat in the Hat*. So I accommodated them.

But the plot quickly thickened.

They were thrilled with the novel concept of my making up a story out of their suggested subjects, and they each wanted to add another component to the *same* story.

It began to become a problem by the third night, when I had to incorporate cheese, a submarine, a frog, a tribe of Indians, a baseball, and a remote-controlled tank.

By the fifth night, they had added a helicopter, a

rubber band, a tiger, and another submarine so there could be a torpedo battle.

So there I sat on night number six.

Sweating.

Twitching.

Muscles tensed.

Mind reeling.

"I can't do this anymore," I said.

"But we like it!" they grinned.

"I'm out of ideas! None of the stories make any sense! I can't do this one more time or I'll scream!"

We went back to *The Cat in the Hat*.

I was in therapy for two years.

On a brighter note, many of the positive routines we initiated early on are still with us today. For instance, we have always prayed before meals. Well, almost always.

On those periodic occasions when Dale or I space out and begin eating before thanking God for our food, one of the boys will inevitably blurt out, "Hey! We didn't pray!"

They then squint at us like we are the most reprobate heathens on the planet.

In a related vein, we make it a practice to meet regularly with other believers to pray, worship, and learn. While Dale and I have no guarantee that our boys will make church an important part of their lives, we are at least building the habit into them.

Some parents get very nervous about requiring church attendance, especially if the kids whine and complain and say they hate it and that if Mom and Dad force it on them they will never go again the split second they move out on their own.

These parents panic. They want their children to *choose* a life of faith, and fear that it will "backfire" if they "force it down their kids' throats."

These are the same parents who, when their kids are toddlers, will wrestle them to the ground and pry open their mouths with a Power Rangers spoon and force liquid Tylenol down their throats no matter how much the kids shriek and wail.

These are also the same parents who will drag Johnny out of bed at 6:45 A.M. Monday through Friday and force him to go to school no matter how much he complains, when what Johnny REALLY wants is to sit in front of the television all day and play video games and eat heaping bowls of sugar.

These parents need to get a grip.

Of COURSE your boys don't want to go to church. They *never* want to do *anything* that is good for them. So ignore what they want and give them what they need. You aren't running for mayor, and you don't have to pander to them.

When Mark was fourteen, he was FURIOUS that Dale and I said he had to attend the church youth group every week.

"I won't participate," he groused. "I am going to sit there and not say anything and no one can make me change."

I checked with the youth group leader, and Mark was being pretty true to his word. He flopped in the back row like a human wet blanket, adding nothing and gaining nothing.

So it seemed.

As time went by, I found that instead of making a

beeline for the car when I came to pick him up, he was waving good-bye to other kids on his way out.

As more time went by, he would be the last one out of the youth room, not the first.

Within a few months, he was bugging *me* to not be late getting him to youth group.

There finally came a day in which Mark was absolutely drowning in homework, and I decided that I needed to cut him some slack. While I really valued the way youth group had become a normal part of his routine, I didn't want him to start resenting it if he was truly overwhelmed with schoolwork.

"Mark," I ventured cautiously as he pored over his books, "I'm not going to make you go tonight if you have too much going on at school."

"Thanks, Dad," he replied. "But there is a core group of us who are trying to see if we can never miss."

I am going to remember that statement LONG after I have forgotten every single line from *The Cat in the Hat*.

When your kid hands you the Crown Jewels of Denmark, it makes an impression.

Chapter 6

Music and Your Boys

—or—

The Revenge of Lawrence Welk

When I was a boy my parents listened to an accordion player named Lawrence Welk every week on a television show sponsored by Geritol (Slogan: "If you have iron-poor blood, this stuff tastes so bad you won't care").

(*Just kidding*, all you Geritol, Inc. attorneys! My editor is extremely concerned about getting sued, so I underscore that the aforementioned slogan is a JOKE.)*

The show featured Mr. Welk, who had some weird Danish or Norwegian accent, introducing a relentlessly smiling group of male and female mannequin-like singers who emitted these terrible songs while he occasionally intruded with an accordion: an instrument so awful that it is actually banned by the United Nations as a weapon of mass destruction.

My parents made all of us kids watch this show.

---

*I think the real slogan was something like "Geritol: A taste that's like—whoa!—better stock up on air-sickness bags!" (That's *another* joke, you corporate attorneys!)

Well, actually, they didn't MAKE us watch it, but it was the only show they would allow on at that particular time slot, so it was the only viewing option, and since we were all glued to the tube whenever it was on, it was ALMOST like they MADE us watch it.

I hated all the music my parents loved. I liked REAL musicians, like the Monkees and other REAL singers who had normal accents and didn't use instruments that were clearly the product of a bizarre foreign government experiment involving a pipe organ and a weather balloon.

This clash of musical tastes created much tension in our home.

"Knock that racket OFF!" my father would roar. "How can you even LISTEN to that garbage? I hope I live to see the day when YOU have to put up with this kind of NOISE from YOUR kids!"

That is what he said when we were simply singing in the shower. He REALLY lost it when we played our records.

I vowed right then and there that I would never be an un-hip parent who made his children listen to awful accordion music. I would allow my kids to listen to the Monkees all they wanted. I would be a cool parent.

Oddly, neither of my boys has shown any interest whatsoever in listening to the Monkees or any of the music I liked when I was younger. You may have noticed that over the past few decades music has taken a sharp turn for the worse. It is this noisy, irritating music my children seem drawn to.

In my day we wouldn't have been caught DEAD listening to rap (even if it existed, which, thank heaven, it did not), which is not really music at all but, rather, semi-intelligible lyrics set to a series of recorded undersea bomb detonations.

Lest you think you are home free simply because the message contained in most rap music is so awful that there is no way on God's green earth you will ever allow it to be played in *your* home, think again. There are, in fact, a few rap groups who have stooped to using positive lyrics for the sole purpose of giving your children a powerful weapon to use against you.

"Gosh, Dad, I never thought you'd prohibit me from listening to 'I Have Decided to Follow Jesus' just because the melody has been updated. . . ."

So I am finding myself—true to my father's curse—fighting with my boys over this jarringly awful noise they dare call music.

They like a group named something like *DC TALK-VERY-LOUD*. This is a "Christian rap group," which to me is just as much an oxymoron as "Presbyterian terrorists."

But because the lyrics are unobjectionable, and actually positive in many ways, we struck a tense truce. Mark and Brad could listen to this cacophony on headphones, but the stereo was reserved for *real* music: defined as "music Dad and Mom grew up listening to."

This worked for a week or two, but headphones do not adequately provide the earthquake-like rumble that rap aficionados crave. So the battle continues.

Only now do I realize where I went wrong.

Your boys will always gravitate toward music you hate.

The only way to avoid this is to begin, when your

boys are very young, listening to music you despise. If I would have listened to Christian rap music when they were toddlers, I believe that today my boys would insist on listening to Bach.

I had been very tempted to finally resolve this dispute by enrolling Mark and Brad in a military academy where they could listen only to patriotic marches, only allowing them to come home once I am an *extremely* senior citizen and deaf. However, we have recently discovered one style of music that we agree on. This has really brought us together as a family.

We all sit around the television once a week watching Lawrence Welk reruns while we make fun of the accordion.

Chapter 7

Hair Wars

—or—

Paying Money to Look Dumb

One day Mark glanced at me and remarked, "You know, if you shaved some of the hair off your arms and pasted it to your forehead you wouldn't look like you are going bald."

He then broke into gales of unbridled mirth and scampered down the hall while I, in a mature and bemused fashion, canceled his allowance for life and attempted to sell him to a circus.

Hair, or the lack of it, is an extremely serious and sensitive issue that should never be joked about by youngsters unless you are me when I was fourteen and you are teasing my dad about the airplanes that may crash from the glare bouncing off his head. Since this cannot be the case, just knock it off this instant.

But even if you, as a dad, are not suffering a hair deficit, the issue of hair will still be a huge source of conflict in your family.

The hair wars will begin quite early in the life of your boys, even before they have any idea that they possess hair. Several months after the birth of your first son, you, the father, will start to get edgy because your wife will not want to cut his beautiful locks and you are mortified at the thought of anyone mistaking him for a girl.

Your wife will think you are overreacting, but you are not. You are simply trying to keep him from being the laughingstock of the town and from suffering severe and prolonged psychological damage, including, but not limited to, gender confusion, delayed sexual development, and the inability to play baseball.

This conflict will eventually be resolved in your favor, but you may have to first resort to covering your son's head with a paper bag whenever you take him out in public. The disagreement with your wife is solved after the first haircut, but, regrettably, the hair battle is not over. It simply shifts to your son.

No little boy likes to sit still for a haircut. He will slouch and twist and whimper while you hover over him with a pair of scissors, sweating like a member of the police bomb squad. You'll manage a little snip here and a little snip there, and forty-five minutes of squirming later you will have succeeded in cutting a total of six hairs. It would be easier to peel the hide off a live badger.

The essential problem is incompatible goals: you want him to look nice, and he wants to play. He does not care what his hair looks like. He does not care if his hair is not cut or shampooed until Mars is colonized. He does not give a whit about dressing nicely for church, or having his shoes on the right feet, or zipping his pants. HE WANTS TO PLAY!

So you will be chasing him around the church parking lot with a comb for several years of your life.

On the positive side, this is great aerobic exercise. Try to make the most of it. This is how many Olympic athletes started out.

One day, you will rise in the morning and put on the coffee and start doing the daily routine and head toward the bathroom to take a shower . . . and you will find that your son is in front of the mirror combing his hair with the fanatical precision of a German auto worker. And you will ask him to leave because you really need to get ready for work and he will turn to you and say, "Can't you see that I'm combing my HAIR?"

He will deliver this line with the same inflection and passion a doctor would employ if he halted traffic on the Golden Gate Bridge and said, "Can't you see I'm delivering TRIPLETS?!!"

From the first day you find one of your sons glued to the bathroom mirror, hair will be the focus of your life for the next decade. This wouldn't be all that bad if your sons were obsessed with looking like wholesome young men who would immediately make an excellent impression on any prospective employer. But they will be spending all this time and energy converting their hair into some ludicrous art form that makes them look like gel-infested aliens.

Psychologists will tell you that stupid, irritating hairstyles are simply signs that your son is trying to find his own identity and define himself apart from his parents. They will also tell you this is harmless and not worth fighting over. They also don't have any children. They have poodles, which also have stupid, irritating haircuts that have been foisted upon them by clueless psychologist owners whom they secretly hate, which explains why they (the poodles) chew up all the good furniture.

Your sons sport stupid hairstyles because their hormones have impacted their vision and they do not realize they look like dorks. This has been documented, and you can test it yourself.

Go find your mom's photo album and see what you looked like in high school. You will agree, I am sure, that the hairstyle you fought with your parents to inflict upon yourself made you look, frankly, like an idiot. You are now mortified by these photos, and you pray that no one will ever see them again.

But back then, you thought you looked GREAT! You thought you looked COOL! Clearly, you were the victim of Hormone Induced Blindness (HIB). It wasn't your fault.

While the underlying cause of stupid adolescent haircuts remains HIB, the condition can manifest itself differently over time. In my younger years, most males chose to grow their hair on the long side, even though our fathers correctly pointed out that we looked like girls (albeit rather ugly girls with excessive facial hair).

While we did look stupid, at least we were in good company. Benjamin Franklin wore his hair long, for example, and he helped draft the Declaration of Independence.

But my sons, and many other boys as of the date of this writing, are willingly adopting a hairstyle so awful that had I been offered the choice as a young person of choosing this haircut or death, I would have instantly flung myself into a cage of starving weasels.

In my worst adolescent nightmare I would wake

up with a haircut that looked as though I had placed a cereal bowl on the top of my head and shaved all the exposed hair down to near baldness. This is precisely the kind of hairstyle my boys PAY to have done to them. The haircut is even called a "bowl cut," so it isn't as though the barbershops are hiding anything.

But your boys are stricken with HIB, and they are absolutely convinced that they look just awesome.

So what are we, as caring and concerned parents, to do?

Dale and I wrestled with this question at great length.

"Dave, I know we don't like their hairstyles, but I think we just need to let them grow out of it," said Dale. "We are going to have more important disagreements down the road, and we need to save our ammunition for those situations where it really matters."

"I guess you're right," I replied reluctantly.

Mark walked into the room just then, hair parted straight down the middle and plastered to his head by sixty-four ounces of gel.

"Mark, your mother and I have decided that it is completely up to you if you want to have a haircut that makes you look like St. Francis of Assisi. That way, you'll be ready to try out for the leading role if the drama club happens to do a play about famous monks who befriended little woodland creatures," I said.

Dale shot a dark look in my direction.

"It could happen," I replied.

Unfortunately, Mark ignored my subtle hint of disapproval and continued to employ the services of a shamelessly unscrupulous barber who would have cheerfully adorned Mark's head with Christmas tinsel as long as he got paid for it.

We try our best to let the Bible serve as the standard for our parental decisions, but the Bible is regrettably silent on the issue of bowl cuts.* When I was younger, Christian parents had the distinct advantage of pointing to 1 Corinthians 11:14, which expressly says that "if a man has long hair, it is a disgrace to him." While it is true that "long" can be a relative term that is open for discussion, at least parents back then had a legitimate basis from which to argue. That moral high ground is lost when your kids insist on cutting their hair far shorter than you ever could have anticipated.

We are stuck with differing over preferences, not revealed truth. And our kids know it. It is just like the debate about music (but without the lyrics, melody, stereo system, musical instruments, or performers).

Some parents choose to simply ignore all of the external issues, like hair and clothing, and instead concentrate on issues of character, morality, and virtue. The beauty of this approach is that it is fairly straightforward to implement as long as you have a severe vision impairment. For the rest of us, it means biting your tongue so hard and so often that you eventually require the services of a speech pathologist.

But Dale has convinced me that this is the wisest approach. Years from now it will not matter that we did not like our boys' hairstyles. But it will matter that

---

*The Bible is also disturbingly silent on the issue of belching, as noted in chapter 2. Why God would not address these two key issues remains a source of intense scholarly debate by theologians who have boys at home.

they became strong Christian men who possess integrity, compassion, courage, and love. Of course, it will also help if they make sure that at least our grandchildren don't look like dorks.

Chapter 8

Morning and Your Boys

—or—

Don't Get Mad, Get Even

Mornings and boys are in some cases not a good mixture, in the sense that cats heaved into a pond are sometimes not a good mixture, or vinegar and a milk shake, or pond water and gruel and motor oil whipped into a blender and poured over warm Spam on toast.

(I'm trying to paint a word picture here.)

Boys operate on a peculiar biological clock, which renders them virtually incapable of getting up on time in the morning unless the morning happens to be Saturday and *Robot Ninja Mutated Penguins* is on television, in which case they can spring instantly out of bed even if it is 3:30 A.M. Otherwise, it takes a crowbar to pry them off the mattress.

This can be a source of frustration for parents, in the sense that having your hair catch on fire can be a source of frustration, or major dental surgery without Novocain, or a combination of flaming hair, dental work, and an IRS audit all at the same time. I hope you are getting the general idea.

I believe that if one of our boys was stricken with a rare sleeping malady and suddenly awoke from a two-year coma, he would hit the snooze alarm and ask for ten extra minutes.

This state of affairs would not pose a problem if we lived in a small and very mellow tropical country where work consisted of cracking open a few coconuts around noonish for lunch. However, we live in the United States of America, where we invented the *atomic clock*, which can count time to within billionths of a second! (One of my former employers owned one of these.) We Americans are serious about time.

Your children cannot make it in this society if their idea of "on time" translates into "give or take a few days." So, once again, it falls to you, the parent, to barge in and build into your boys a strong sense of the importance of punctuality. Otherwise, they may grow up to be listless high school dropouts who sit around playing with computers all day creating revolutionary software programs that IBM purchases for sixty-two million dollars, thus enabling them to buy that little tropical country we were talking about and then lie around in a hammock all day while paying the natives to open the coconuts for them, which would rob them of the chance to develop this valuable skill on their own.

No, you must work hard to spare them from this fate.

"But, Dave," you may say, "I have been fighting for YEARS to get my kids out of the house and to school on time, but nothing works! What possible technique could you have developed that none of us other hapless and bungling parents has tried?"

I'm glad you asked, for this is where I outline for you the extraordinary results achieved by what my wife has termed "The Ice Cubes of Happiness" (patent pending).

"But, Dave," you may say, "surely you don't mean that you attempt to wake your kids up with a standard alarm clock and then count to five and if they don't get out of bed you put ice cubes in their beds?"

Of course not. I am not *completely* heartless. Very often, I will count all the way to ten.

The results have been splendid. The problem is no longer one of nagging them to get up, but of sneaking into their rooms quietly enough to prevent them from bolting out of bed before I even have the chance to pop the ice cubes out of the tray.

"Wow, Dave!" you may exclaim. "This piece of advice alone is worth the price of this book! I am going to recommend your book to all of my friends and it will probably become a bestseller and you will become unbelievably wealthy! What will you do with all that money?"

For starters, I will work on my tan.

Somebody pass me a coconut.

And throw that clock away.

Chapter 9

A Glitch in Time

In the bowels of Washington, D.C., is a small building that houses the Federal Bureau of Ridiculous Policies. Their job is to come up with national "April Fools" gags, such as the income tax code and daylight saving time.

Our willingness to participate in these pranks makes me wonder if we are all being reduced to the mental equivalent of unquestioningly obedient wiener dogs—albeit with the ability to still pay taxes.

Like lemmings marching dutifully into the sea, more than one hundred million otherwise rational parents—grown people who would never believe an Elvis sighting or be conned into eating tofu—do not even pause to ask Aristotle's age-old question, "Just why am I **doing** this, anyway?" as they obediently set their clocks forward one hour, then back again a few months later, **simply because some obscure federal agency said to do so.**

Don't you feel **embarrassed** at having fallen for this enormous federal gag, the government's version of a "Kick Me" sign taped to our collective derriere?

Children are not so easily conned, as I learned from Brad one day.

"What are you doing?" he asked as I moved from room to room, changing all the clocks.

I explained that I was "springing forward" to make up for having "fallen back" several months ago, which, in turn, was a reaction to having "sprung forward" the previous year, but only because I had also "fallen back" even earlier than that.

"Oh," he replied and watched patiently while I agitatedly mumbled my way though the manual for the VCR timer, the microwave, the digital clock-radio, and both automobile clocks, which, by the time I finished, simply blinked "00:00."

"But what time is it **really**?" he finally asked.

Hmmm.

Not wishing to appear hopelessly deficient in the chronology department, I attempted to explain that, according to a famous scientist named Albert Einstein, who spent his life developing and proving elaborate theories like "$E=mc^2$" and "A Stitch in Time Saves Nine," it was, currently, time for bed.

"But it's only seven-thirty," he protested, pointing to his watch and casting a deeply suspicious glance at the clock I had just rehung on the living room wall.

"I know," I replied. "But we have to treat it like it's eight-thirty because, um . . . well . . ."

"You mean you just changed all the clocks and now we have to **pretend** what time it is?" he asked with a furrowed brow. "Why didn't you just leave them alone?"

Thus began several weeks of open warfare between myself and Bradley. He wouldn't get up on time, because time had lost all meaning for him. If I was just going to spin the hands on the clock to apparently suit my whims, he was not going to play along. As far as he knew, the next logical step was to change months and perhaps skip his birthday. Why didn't I just rewrite the Ten Commandments while I was at it?

"Brad, you have to finish those Rice Krispies or you are going to be late to school!" I would say.

"Yeah, right," he would mumble. "I still have a whole HOUR in REAL time!"

Getting him to bed on time had always been difficult, but I had always held the upper hand because, as much as he wanted to stay up past his bedtime, the term "bedtime" was objective. He could plead for more minutes, but at least the minutes had an understood meaning. Not anymore. As far as he was concerned, time had all the rigidity of a rubber band.

Ultimately, peace was restored when I simply put my foot down as the head of my household and changed his bedtime to nine o'clock (in real time). This compromise meant that he was actually adding only thirty minutes to his real bedtime, but the clock said he was going to bed an hour and a half later than he was used to, unless I am confused and I accidentally added ninety minutes to his real bedtime, which would factor out to two and a half hours in daylight saving time, in which case I have, once again, been made a fool of by the Bureau of Ridiculous Policies.

Thomas Jefferson said that a little rebellion now and then is a good thing. Easy for him to say, living as he did in an era when "now and then" actually meant something. Given our contemporary allegiance to daylight saving time, we have absolutely no clue as to whether "now" is, in fact, "then" or "then" is, in reality, "now." And it gets even worse when you fly across a time zone or take a nighttime cold medicine.

Perhaps daylight saving time is actually a malevolent government plot created to prevent us from acting upon Jefferson's sage advice because we are preoccupied with arguing with our boys about their real bedtime.

Well, I say we end these stupid government pranks no matter **what** time it is. We parents aren't going to take it anymore! We have enough trouble with getting our kids to bed on time without having the government conspire against us! Let's march on the Capitol!

Plan to meet promptly at, um, well . . . drat!

Chapter 10

Pets and Your Boys

—or—

In Praise of Stuffed Toys

A dog can offer your boys a host of valuable learning opportunities, such as: learning to be drooled upon, learning to pretend you are vision impaired when it is your turn to do pooper-scooper duty, and learning to watch your parents fork over prodigious wads of cash to the veterinarian when the dog eats the neighbor kid's new seventy-five-dollar sneakers.

In addition to the aforementioned benefits, a dog can make an excellent twenty-four-hour guard against intruders unless your dog happens to be ours, in which case it will mistake you for the intruder and attempt to remove your lymph nodes.

Our dog is a sweet mutt named "Pepper," who is extremely devoted to our family. She is also a complete buffoon, who nearly killed me one fateful summer afternoon. If grass had an IQ, Pepper's would be even lower.

We did not set out to adopt a dog like Pepper. I had originally planned to carefully study up on all the major flavors of dog and pick a mellow, obedient, shed-resistant, potty-trained, computer-literate breed.

I gave more thought to this choice than I normally do for picking a senator.

Regrettably, we happened one day to be visiting some friends who live out in the country with their gaggle of cats, dogs, birds, and assorted children when they remarked, IN FRONT OF OUR BOYS, that they had an extra puppy. She was a stray and they were just going to have to take her to the (PAUSE FOR OMINOUS CELLO MUSIC) dog pound if someone wouldn't adopt her.

Little eyes stared up at me imploringly.

I could either go down in history as the Compassionate Rescuer of the Forlorn Puppy, or I could be remembered as the Evil Communist Traitor Father Who Sent the Poor Puppy to Siberia.

So Pepper came home with us. She was a walking ball of lint, with hair that would shed by the handfuls the moment she engaged in any form of strenuous activity, such as blinking.

You could make fifty rugs with the hair that covers our backyard (but only if you are into rugs that smell like a dead elk. More on this in the section titled "Interesting Smells That Dogs and Boys Will Get Into").

Fortunately, Pepper has some very good qualities. I mentioned earlier that she is very devoted to our family, and she is fiercely protective when she spies an approaching danger, such as the United Parcel Service driver. She barks every time the United Parcel Service truck comes down our street, which HAPPENS FIVE TIMES A WEEK, thus alerting us to the looming prospect that, EVEN THOUGH THE UNITED PARCEL SERVICE DRIVER HAS NEVER DONE

ANYTHING TO US IN THE PRIOR 987 TIMES
HE HAS DRIVEN DOWN OUR STREET, *this time
he just may be a member of an extremist faction* intent
on delivering a nuclear weapon to our mailbox, and
only the aggressive yapping of Pepper will make him
think twice.

So we have much to be thankful for.

We can also thank Pepper for saving us the cost of
adding a "doggy door" to the back door of our garage,
because she literally *ate a hole through it* the first time
we had a thunderstorm. She then saved us the cost of
a doghouse because she refuses to leave the garage at
night lest doing so will cause the thunder to return.

We can also thank Pepper for saving me from dangerous barbecue apparel. In fact, back in the days
when I was researching precisely what brand of dog to
acquire, obtaining protection from dangerous barbecue apparel was high on my priority list.

Pepper displayed this crucial quality one day when
I donned my barbecue apron and ventured forth into
the backyard. The apron, given to me by my mother-
in-law, is a bold orange-and-black checkered pattern
emblazoned with the command to "Kiss the Cook."
The word "Cook" is embellished so that there are eye-
lashes above and pupils inside the two "o's."

I was making my way toward the barbecue when
Pepper bounded toward me for our favorite ritual in
which she plasters her dirty paws on my chest while I
yell at her to "SIT!"

She was in midbound when she spotted those huge
and foreign eyes on the apron, and she knew
INSTINCTIVELY that this had something to do with
the "evil" United Parcel Service driver. She lunged—a

snarling, snapping blur of rapidly shedding hair.

Utilizing every lesson I had ever learned about animal control, I flailed at her with my barbecue mitt and screamed, "It's ME, you IDIOT!"

She paused, looked up at my face, wagged her tail, then looked back at those assassin's eyes and renewed the attack.

"Down, you IMBECILE!" I commanded.

She paused again, and you could see her mind racing.

"Yes," she said to herself, "the voice belongs to the guy who buys my Kibbles 'n' Bits, but I must destroy this madman before he touches the detonator!"

I was chased from my own backyard.

Pepper sat by the barbecue, a smug "I told you so!" look on her face as the chicken went up in flames.

Unlike a goldfish, you cannot simply flush a dog down the toilet when it begins to get on your nerves. If you do not own a dog, you probably don't realize just how much a part of your life they become. When you bring a dog home, you have essentially adopted a new member into the family.

While Pepper will always be a buffoon, she will always be *our* buffoon. You could not buy her from us even if (for some inexplicable reason) you wanted to. For better or for worse, she is family.

There is no terribly objective reason why Pepper is a part of our life. It isn't as though she rescued one of the kids from a burning building or anything. No, she was just one more stray dog in a world with millions of stray dogs. But we elected to take her home, to love her, and to make her ours. In a small way, we exercised a virtue known as "grace." That is, we extended an unearned favor on someone who would otherwise have faced a grim future.

In response to the affection we have lavished on Pepper, she absolutely adores us. She jumps and barks and wags her tail at speeds approaching 100 mph every time we return from even a short trip, such as to the bathroom. She will play relentlessly with us, pausing only to dash to the fence and bark at any perceived threat. If any package-delivery-service terrorist ever decides to kidnap one of the boys, it will be over Pepper's dead body.

I asked Mark and Brad one day why Pepper loves us. "Do you think she is trying to pay us back?" I asked.

Brad shook his head. "She doesn't think about it," he replied.

"She just loves us because we love her," Mark said.

We came to the conclusion that neither Pepper, nor any other dog, understands the concept of obligation, or debt, or quid pro quo. Pepper is not attempting to pay us back. She knows she is "ours" in the most positive sense of that word, and she simply responds to that love and care with whatever the dog version of "love" happens to be.

In this sense, a dog can help your boys understand something about God's love toward us.

We, too, are "strays." Like Pepper, we are all heading for a grim future unless someone rescues us. And like a stray, we have no way to earn this adoption into a new home. Of course, the analogy completely falls apart because none of us dies for the sins of his pet, like Jesus died for the sins of the world (and arose from the grave once His mission was completed!).

But we can still teach our kids an important lesson from the key point that we *do not earn our relationship with our Master, nor do we pay Him back.* We simply enjoy the incredible privilege of adoption and respond very naturally with love and loyalty.

And unlike my rule with Pepper, God will actually let us sit on the good furniture—not because we have earned the right, but just because He is far kinder than any of us can possibly comprehend.

That lesson is worth all the vet bills.

Chapter 11

Your Boys—Are They Truly Clueless or Just Ignoring You?

A huge portion of your son's life will consist of your supplying him with detailed information that he will not understand, but that you will think he understands because he will nod as you speak to him and even repeat back to you verbatim everything you said while never understanding a word of it.

What your son *does* understand is that (1) pretending to understand means he can go outside and play *much* sooner than if he hangs around to seek clarification; (2) gaining clarification usually means that he has to do something he does not really want to do anyway; and (3) you will ultimately forgive him if he apologizes, even if he is only vaguely aware of exactly what it is for which he is apologizing.

Sometimes your boys will not understand because they refuse to invest the effort in trying to understand, and at other times they will honestly think they understand but simply do not. Since the end result is the same (they don't do what you ask them to do), you will be hugely frustrated—especially if you are the kind of parent who believes that a child's *motivation* for disobedience is the key factor in determining an appropriate disciplinary response. It is justice to punish disobedience; it is futile to punish cluelessness.

EXAMPLE: You receive a call that some friends will be dropping by your home shortly. You tell your son that before he runs off to play he must fold the laundry (strewn all over the couch), which takes about fifteen minutes, but he instead takes out the trash, which takes two minutes, and which you do not observe him doing.

"Can I go now?" he calls from another room as you tidy up the kitchen.

"Did you finish your job?" you ask.

"Yes."

"OK. Bye."

Moments later the doorbell rings and you discover that the unsightly mound of clothing is still lounging on your couch like a bloated, defiant "Jabba the Hutt" space alien. So you seize the rumpled shirts and shorts and fling them into your son's room where—YOU JUST BETTER BELIEVE IT!—he will do them later and then you lunge for the door and try to act cool and calm and collected and mature while all you can *really* think about is getting your best friends OUT of your house as soon as possible so you can dismantle your son's video game and flush the parts down the toilet one by one because he is NOT going to get away with this kind of flagrant disobedience and dishonesty!

When your son finally moseys in the door an hour later you are a frothing, incoherent glob of righteous indignation.

"I don't know WHO you think you are, young man, but when you tell me you have finished a job IT HAD BETTER BE FINISHED, and don't you EVER [*froth, froth, indignation, more froth*] . . ." But your sputtering fit of vexation is slowly extinguished by the look of absolute puzzlement on the face of your son.

"But I did take out the garbage!" he will reply with a furrowed brow.

Uh-oh.
Shades of gray.
Possible misunderstanding.
Guilt Alert!

He could have meant to obey but simply misunderstood or just spaced out for a moment. On the other hand, he could have just decided that taking out the garbage was quicker and easier, and he is risking that you will buy his explanation.

Instead of meting out punishment, you have to rapidly decide (1) whether he is clever enough and dishonest enough to have pulled a "bait and switch" on you, or (2) whether you should put the replacement video system on your VISA or just write a check.

Some parents confuse almost all *failure to understand* with *disobedience*, but they are wrong. These parents simply cannot believe that their VERY CLEAR AND DETAILED INSTRUCTIONS could have been misunderstood, so they accuse the child of defiance and having a snotty attitude and send him to his room and ground him for life.

Listen, I am the *last* one to make excuses for defiance and snottiness, but I have learned over time that, as unbelievable as it seems, boys really can be far more clueless than you would ever imagine possible.

This will become clear to you once you observe them doing something that is glaringly absurd and clearly against their own best interests and then coming to you stunned and bewildered about it.

EXAMPLE: When Brad was quite young he asked to borrow our expensive camera for a class field trip to the zoo. We thought that was risky, so we bought him one of those disposable cameras instead. We carefully explained how to use it and sent him on his way.

He returned home very excited about the pictures he had taken.

"But how do they get the pictures to you?" he asked. "How do they know where I live?"

Since it was a disposable camera, he had dutifully tossed it into a trash can at the zoo.

So you can't automatically rule out "failure to get the concept" when you are trying to get dinner ready and you ask your son to put the glasses on the table and a few minutes later you discover your sunglasses sitting by your plate.

If your sons only did stupid stuff when you asked them to do a job, you could safely reason that they are simply playing an unamusing game with you. But when you watch your high-schooler sweat bullets half the night and cram for a major test only to discover that he is one week too early, you realize that you are not dealing with a good listener.

The fact still remains, however, that sometimes your sons will misunderstand you because they are just tuning you out. Some famous communication experts suggest that both you and your children learn to repeat back whatever has just been said in order to ensure that you really understand each other. These experts also suggest that you take the lead by modeling the behavior, as outlined in the following conversation.

EXAMPLE:

Mark: "I don't think you and Mom really listen to me."

Me: "It sounds to me like you think Mom and I don't really listen to you."

Mark: "Why do you always repeat everything I say? It drives me nuts! Do you have Alzheimer's or what?"

So much for the experts.

Even if you can get your son to parrot back exactly what you told him, like some kind of human videocassette, it doesn't mean he will retain any of it for more than fifteen seconds. Videocassettes can be recorded over, and so can your son's memory.

EXAMPLE:

Me: "Mark, I want you to clean up your room right now!"

Mark: "Can I finish reading the chapter I'm on first? It is at an exciting part."

Me: "No. Just get your job out of the way before all our company arrives."

Mark: "Please?"

Me: "No. You need to learn to just focus and get something done in a timely manner. This is part of learning the work ethic. If I let you keep reading, it would take you forever to get this done."

Mark:	"OK."
Me:	"So you are going to stop reading and clean up your room. Repeat back to me what I said."
Mark:	"I am going to stop reading and clean up my room."

One hour later, I walk into his messy room and he is still reading.

Me:	"WHAT ARE YOU DOING??!! I TOLD YOU AN HOUR AGO TO CLEAN UP THIS ROOM!!!"
Mark:	"I thought you said I could focus on my book as long as I didn't take forever to get my room done." Pause. "And something about ethics."

And he sounds so completely sincere that I wonder exactly what it was I said. Maybe I *do* have Alzheimer's.

Misunderstanding also commonly occurs when your son thinks he already knows what you are going to say, so he is occupied with forming a response rather than listening to what you are actually saying. While it is still a form of tuning you out, it is not necessarily deliberate. If I say, "Jack and Jill ran up the hill," your mind will instantly complete the phrase "to fetch a pail of water."

Likewise, your boys know all your stock phrases.

"Stop fiddling with that pencil before you—*(poke someone's eye out)*."

"Money doesn't—*(grow on trees)*."

"Close that door! Were you—*(born in a barn?)*"

The point is, there are some phrases our kids have heard so many times that they do, in fact, know what we are about to say.

You can usually tell when this kind of misunderstanding is occurring because your son will almost inevitably complete your sentence for you.

EXAMPLE:

You: "Son, about the—"

Son: "Science project. I know. I'm already working on it, and you and Mom don't have to monitor every single thing I do."

You: "Hey! Cool the attitude! I wasn't even remotely thinking about your science project, but I did want to mention—"

Son: "The dog needs to be fed. You don't need to remind me. I was just going to do it."

You: "As a matter of fact, I was NOT going to talk about the dog. I was merely going to point out that—"

Son: "You want the lawn mowed. Well, I can't get that done unless you cut me some slack about the science project and the dog!"

You: "STOP INTERRUPTING ME OR I'LL DISMANTLE YOUR VIDEO GAME INTO LITTLE PIECES AND—"

Son: "Flush them down the toilet. I can read your and Mom's minds. Don't you get tired of giving the plumber all your money?"

At this point, you might be tempted to give up any hope of ever achieving clear and meaningful communication with your boys. (I certainly am.)

But before we are too quick to despair over our

boys' rampant and continuing misunderstandings of us, it might be instructive to recall that even Jesus' disciples misunderstood Him on a regular basis (and not just when He was speaking in parables, which they *never* understood). If adults could misunderstand Jesus, a uniquely gifted communicator, it should not be all that surprising that kids can misunderstand parents.

EXAMPLE:

In the gospel account recorded in Luke, we read the following:

"And He took the twelve aside and said to them, 'Behold, we are going up to Jerusalem, and all things which are written through the prophets about the Son of Man will be accomplished. For He will be delivered to the Gentiles, and will be mocked and mistreated and spit upon, and after they have scourged Him, they will kill Him; and the third day He will rise again'" (18:31–33 NIV).

That was about as clear and concise a summary as Jesus could have possibly conveyed to His disciples.

"We are going to JERUSALEM, where I will be delivered up to the GENTILES and I will be mocked and mistreated and KILLED, but THREE DAYS later I will RISE FROM THE DEAD."

The issue is not whether the disciples welcomed the message Jesus gave them, but whether the message was clear.

It sounds clear to me.

However, the VERY NEXT sentence says, "And they understood none of these things. . . ."

None?

Not a word?

How could they NOT understand Him? Which part of what Jesus said was not clear? Was it the part about going up to Jerusalem? Did they think he said Bethlehem, or Samaria, or *Chicago*, for that matter?

Or was it the part about being mocked, mistreated, and killed? Are there too many shades of gray to get the drift of those words?

Was the concept of "three days" too complex to grasp? Did they think he said "twenty-seven" or "two hundred and sixty"?

Were these guys so dense they couldn't understand plain Aramaic?

I think the key reason they did not understand is that they thought they already understood. This is precisely the problem that kids often have with their parents (and that husbands and wives have with each other, as well).

It is pretty obvious from some of the other conversations the Bible records about the disciples that they expected Jesus to enter Jerusalem in triumph, stomp the Romans, and set up a new kingdom. They had already been jockeying for the key positions of power in the new order.

What Jesus actually said was extremely plain and easy to understand, but His statement was in such contrast to their expectations—what they just "knew" to be true—that His words literally went right over their heads. "They understood none of these things."

They were listening, but they weren't hearing.

While I was in the process of writing this chapter, I overheard the following conversation between Dale and Mark (I am not kidding—talk about perfect timing):

Mark: "I know you always say 'no' before dinner, but just this once I would like to have my pie first because I was too full to have it last night after dinner and everyone else had theirs and I am getting cheated."

Dale: "Well . . ."

Mark: "Before you say anything, just realize that everyone else will keep having it and it is already mostly gone and I am getting ripped off. So please? Just this time?"

Dale: "OK."

Mark: "Why can't you stop being so strict all the time?!"

Dale: "I SAID 'OK'! WHAT PART OF 'YES' DON'T YOU UNDERSTAND?"

Mark: "So can I have some?"

This kid is definite disciple material.

But while it is easy to criticize the disciples as particularly dense, I am not much different. I have been a Christian for many years now, and I have read much of the Bible a good many times. But often I discover something staggeringly important that I have missed on a hundred prior readings.

You see, a huge portion of my life has consisted of God supplying me with detailed information, that I did not understand but that I thought I understood and even repeated back to Him verbatim while never really understanding it. Sometimes I have not understood because I did not invest the effort in trying to understand, and at other times I thought I truly understood but simply did not.

Sound familiar?

We all need to listen until we truly understand. It was true for the disciples, it is true for our kids, and it goes for us as well. Before we get too frustrated with the kids, we need to assess our own listening skills.

The Bible says we should be "quick to listen, slow to speak and slow to become angry" (James 1:19 NIV).

Interestingly, when we truly listen to our boys—look them in the eye and truly hear them—they tend to truly listen to us as well.

As an added bonus, we will save LOTS of money on video games and plumbing expenses.

Chapter 12

Camping with Boys

—or—

If God Had Intended Us to Live in the Forest, He Wouldn't Have Given Us Mortgage Bankers

From earliest human history, people have devised a variety of ingenious ways to protect themselves against the ravages of nature. Clothes can range from a simple loin-cloth to fashion-designer outfits (in some cases, they are one and the same), and homes can encompass everything from huts and igloos to apartments and mansions.

In every case, people are responding to a basic human need to protect their bodies from the elements as they go about their day and to have a shelter to return to when they see danger approaching, such as a life insurance salesman.

Americans have always tended toward sturdy and spacious structures whenever possible. We are not a nomadic people living in tents and hunkering down over fires. This is mostly because the Pilgrims, after suffering through those wretched early years, had seen enough of snow, wind, pouring rain, suffocating heat, and swarms of insects to last five lifetimes and embarked on a building spree that continues to this very day.

If they could look down upon us now, I am sure that they would be astonished at what we have wrought. We not only shelter ourselves from the elements in houses and condominiums, but we can also control our indoor climate through the use of air conditioners. We can store refrigerated food in our kitchens and create instant dinners in microwave ovens. In short, we have largely overcome all the physical hardships they endured.

Yes, the Pilgrims would indeed be impressed—until they noticed that millions of us regularly abandon our safe and comfortable homes in the heat of SUMMER and drive to FORESTS that are absolutely jammed with WILDLIFE and INSECTS where we sleep in TENTS on the GROUND and hunker over FIRE PITS fueled by FLAMING MARSHMALLOWS and try to catch FISH which we then have to GUT when we have Heat & Serve Pasta at home in the FREEZER. And these Pilgrims would give one another incredulous looks and say things like, "Canst thou believest thine eyes, William? Our progeny, for which we hath risked life and limb, are idiots and *buffoons!*"

And we are!

Not only are grown people—many of whom are not alcoholics—willingly venturing out into an unpredictable and dangerous environment, which in a great many cases lacks showers, but in the overwhelming number of cases we are taking our boys!

RECIPE FOR DISASTER: Mix active boys with dirt, a cold stream, pinecones, sap, and chipmunks. Stir in three cans of OFF! brand mosquito repellent, cold scrambled eggs, syrup, expensive binoculars, and pillows. Zip into sleeping bags and add spooky animal sounds. Allow to rise at 4:30 A.M. without changing their clothes. Whip coffee into adults. Repeat until rainstorm arrives. Finished when adults do not respond when poked with a toothpick.

No matter how many times we do this, we keep coming back for more. I think that trees must give off some judgment-impairing chemical that keeps us returning again and again. Perhaps we pollinate the forest without knowing it.

Whatever the case, Dale and I also flung common sense to the wind one year (it was blowing northeast, as I recall) and drove to Lake Almanor in northern California when Mark and Brad were ages seven and five.

The kids really wanted to fish, and I really wanted to fish, which was a perfect situation, except for the fact that we had completely different definitions of what it meant to fish.

To me, "fishing" means a quiet couple of hours casting lures into a calm and quiet lake. It is a time to soak in the scenery, shed the tension of the city, and entice a trout to strike at a flashing bit of metal.

To Mark and Brad, "fishing" meant a maximum of four casts, and unless they caught something, they were going to throw rocks in the water, or wade, or chase a chipmunk, or look for snakes, or any of one hundred options that did not include shedding the tension of the city and soaking up the calm and quiet scenery. Additionally, each cast by a young boy turns immediately into an enormous project rivaling a space shuttle launch (only with much more monofilament).

FISHING GEAR TIP: When fishing with young boys you can save hours and hours of time by, first thing when you arrive at the water's edge, ripping handfuls of monofilament from the spools and shaking fifty-seven lures into the resulting ball of line. The amateurs tend to dink around for half the day before they arrive at this point. You might just as well get it over and be done with it.

So we didn't catch any fish; nor did we shed much tension or soak up much scenery. We did, however, soak up a lot of water.

I had purchased a four-person raft to go with our four-person tent. In both cases, the manufacturer must have meant "four person" to mean "two sets of Siamese twins" or "four people with a drastic genetic disorder rendering them all the size of wiener dogs."

We squeezed into the raft and paddled around the lake for a while until the kids were cold. We made it safely back to shore, but somehow, employing roughly the same physical law that says when one person jumps off the teeter-totter the other person is going to have an unpleasant landing, the minute the kids jumped onto the shore, Dale was unceremoniously dumped into a very cold body of water. At least the kids had the maturity to make sure she was OK before they started laughing, so I guess that is a good sign.

We hauled her from the lake and covered her with blankets in the car while I attempted to erect the tent.

The packaging on our tent said that it was a "dome" style, but "dome" actually meant "about the size of a large umbrella." Always the optimist, Dale said that it would look much better once it was set up. (She didn't realize that it **was** set up. When it **wasn't** set up, it looked like a deflated beach ball punctured by four bent BIC pens.)

By the time we fit in Mark's and Brad's sleeping bags, shoes, jammies, stuffed toys, and sizable plastic weapons arsenal, there was no room for us. (Our children had a pathological, almost hysterical fear of the dark, hence the dependence on weapons. Their pediatrician said they would have outgrown it much sooner if I had not kept telling them scary stories at night.)

I tried to convince Dale that it would be fun to sleep out in the open with no tent barring our view of the stars. After breaking into a gale of sustained laughter and rolling around on the ground while pointing at me, she elected to fold down the backseats of the station wagon and sleep in the car. She was not deterred by my observation that she looked like a vagrant.

Actually, I would have joined her, but we had to leave all the food boxes and coolers inside the car to discourage bears from invading. There was no room for me. So she cuddled up to the picnic basket while I drifted off to sleep beneath the Big Dipper, nestled comfortably in the four-wiener-dog raft.

Actually, "drifted off to sleep" is not quite accurate. Drifted merrily downstream is more like it. A sudden, raging rainstorm sent a small river through our camp, dousing the fire and turning my sleeping bag into a gargantuan sponge. And the zipper was jammed. I abandoned the raft and lurched toward the car. It was locked. And Dale is a sound sleeper. Either that or she was getting back at me for comparing her to a hobo.

I tapped on the windows, thumped the door panels, rocked the car back and forth, shouted apologies, promised to go to the fabric store without rolling my eyes or yawning—a bomb blast wouldn't have elicited a yawn from her. So I waded back into the river and made toward the kids' tent.

Looking back on it now, I realize that telling them that spooky story before bedtime was not the best of all possible entertainment choices. I didn't want to wake them, so I did not announce myself as I crawled slowly into the tent. That proved to be a costly lapse in judgment. All they knew was that the slimy Sponge Creature from Neptune was slowing oozing into their tent.

I am still not quite sure what hit me, but the nurse assured me that I will regain most of my limb function after I complete all of the physical therapy.

After that kind of forest experience, you may be wondering why on earth Dale and I have the gumption and courage (a.k.a. foolishness and brain damage) to even venture out onto our front lawn.

In two words: desperate optimism.

Like most parents, we are desperate optimists. We have to be. All parents operate on the premise, wholly without any basis in empirical evidence, that things *have* to get better.

Oh sure, the campfire may have gotten a little out of control *last* time when one of the kids decided to "encourage" the flames by squirting charcoal lighter fluid directly onto the coals and then panicking when the flames started to race toward the bottle and so he dropped the entire twenty-four ounces of highly combustible fluid right into the fire and the burgers literally launched off the grill and are now stuck to a NASA satellite, but *surely* things will be better next time.

Optimism, even in the face of today's reality, is the mainstay of parenthood. Without it, we would be hysterical and insane and make appearances on daytime television talk shows alongside the people who believe the moon is really a massive interstellar cotton ball and all of our cosmetic puffs are actually alien life forms.

If you are a parent, and have ever taken your kids out to a restaurant with another family, and your kids simply *could not* stop making faces at each other or blowing bubbles in their drinks or playing footsie under the table or giggling at other patrons, you have more than likely been so embarrassed that you quietly vowed—between sharp, quick commands of "stop it right this instant!"—that you are NEVER taking them out to dinner again. But you did anyway.

Was it because there was a sudden and profound change in your children? Was it because you one day awoke to the sight of your boys waxing the kitchen floor and placing fresh flowers on the breakfast table and saying, in charming British accents, "Good morning, dearest Mother! How might we make this a pleasant day for you?" (If the answer is yes, they either broke something expensive or they want money.)

No, you took them out again because you said to yourself, "They wouldn't dare do that to me again."

That is what I mean by desperate optimism. It isn't just about camping or going out to dinner. It is about getting out of bed every day. It is about the whole prospect of raising kids.

The hope that things will all work out and our boys will grow up to be decent, thoughtful, caring, and responsible Christian men—even though, just an hour ago, they were trying to find out if the fence would catch on fire from just the beam of a magnifying glass (the answer is yes)—is the thin thread on which we hang our fondest dreams. We boldly, audaciously assume that our kids will someday become mature adults capable of being entrusted with the task of raising their own children and running the country and safely using a Black and Decker power saw because children are a gift from the Lord and, unlike with Sears, *you are not allowed to return them even if you have a receipt.*

There is no turning back. God has landed you on the wild shore called parenthood, and if you turn around you will notice He has set a torch to the ship that brought you there.

Our optimism, although sometimes tinged with desperation, springs from our assurance that God is good and that His grace, coupled with our tears, prayers, and hard work, can prevail in the end.

Yep. Those little munchkins who insisted on bringing home a bucket of extremely deceased and fragrant crayfish found on the beach are the same souls God desires to be the leaders of tomorrow. If we lose hope, if we fail to do our part as parents, we not only endanger the next generation, but we might just as well kiss off Social Security.

We are attempting to do with our boys what the Pilgrims did with their new land. We are taming nature.

Camping is almost a metaphor for that. The tent represents a safe place in the world you create for your kids. The campfire represents the basic human passions that need to be both coaxed and controlled. And the flaming marshmallows represent your need for a substantial liability insurance policy.

Chapter 13

Sound Fiscal Planning (and Other Quaint Myths)

"Money management" is a vitally important life skill to learn and to pass on to your children, and with thoughtful planning and discipline it can be surprisingly simple to implement as long as you are the king of Switzerland. For those of us who are not rulers of wealthy nations, "money management" is a myth right up there with Big Foot and alien abductions (but less believable).

I absolutely loathe money-management lectures, workbooks, charts, videotapes, and assorted paraphernalia, and I *especially* loathe the finger-pointing, bean-counting, sanctimonious little "I'm-more-prudent-than-you" accountant trolls who make me feel dense and guilty and irresponsible and doomed. If I sound a little testy, it is only because I am writing this late at night after I have just paid all the bills. The only money I have left to "manage" is the change in the ashtray of my aging Ford station wagon. One dollar and sixty-seven cents, to be exact.

According to the money-management experts, at

this point in my life I should have a balanced portfolio consisting of mutual funds, growth stocks, and six months' worth of income invested in a readily accessible "liquid" account.

I don't.

Rather, I have invested heavily in orthodontic services, Froot Loops, and my boys' basketball shoes.

But the smug little trolls, on the other hand, are all mailing sizable checks each month to investment companies like "Mutually Prudent People Who Live in Omaha." All of the mutually prudent people live in Omaha, where there is really nothing to do with your money except purchase wheat by the boxcar. Once the novelty of that wears off, they amass large quantities of cash, which they cram into grain elevators until there is no more room. They finally resort to lending excess loot to people like me in the form of VISA cards with exorbitant interest rates.

I used to sort of admire the fiscally prudent people, with their foresight and self-restraint and plans for the future. But that was before I realized that there are no "Six Flags Over the Wheat Fields" theme parks, or anything *else* to spend money on in the grain-infested state of Nebraska. So it isn't like they are really any better or smarter than the rest of us; it's just that they don't have a lot of material temptations in Omaha.

But making fun of financially secure people will not change the fact that my own finances are hardly in stellar shape. I would feel guilty enough if I were alone in this mess, but I am a parent and I am supposed to be modeling all kinds of virtues for my boys, including financial responsibility.

For a long time I tried to fake fiscal responsibility

in the expectation of eventually achieving it, desperately hoping that no one would catch on before I succeeded in getting my fiscal house in order. (Hey, Congress got away with this for *years* until Newt and Associates took over.)

But fakery has its limits, especially as your kids get older and start wising up.

Me: "Mark, let's discuss prudent financial management today. The habits you make here and now will serve as the foundation for your financial future. Let's do a role play; I'll pretend to be the customer and you will be the lending institution."

Mark: "Let me guess. You need gas money again until you get paid."

Me: "Ha, ha, ha! What a jokester! This is a training exercise for *your* benefit, you little comedian."

Mark: "It will cost you 30 percent interest, compounded daily."

Me: "That's highway robbery! Not even Louie the loan shark charges that much! I checked!"

Mark: "Hey, anyone who needs to consistently borrow money from a minor is a credit risk. I figure I am doing you a favor at anything less than a rate of 50 percent. Pay me back by next week or I'll report your account as delinquent."

Me: "You know, Jesus drove people like you out of the temple with a whip."

Mark: "I donate a percentage of the profits I make off you to the church. How else do you think they could have funded the remodeling of the youth center? Talk about a win-win situation."

Providing this kind of "hands-on" training in money management can help your children grasp the importance of financial planning.

I call it "Reverse Illustration."

"Don't be like me, and one day you could be the king of Switzerland" is the message I give my children.

Maybe they will be so grateful that they will let me live with them someday in their spacious mansions in Nebraska.

Chapter 14

Impersonal Responsibility

The willingness and capacity to accept personal responsibility is absolutely foundational to your son's mental health and emotional maturity. Our basic, sinful human tendency is to cut ourselves all kinds of slack to avoid facing the fact that if we are free to make choices, we are also responsible for the choices we make (unless chocolate is involved, in which case we get into the thorny issue of "free will vs. predestination").

But I digress.

One of the most powerful and important lessons a father can teach his son—and this could literally someday save his life—can be summed up in just five words: "Put the toilet seat down."

My wife MADE me put that in. What this chapter is REALLY supposed to be about is the *following* five-word lesson: "Take responsibility for your choices."

Your boy will not truly become a man until he is willing to take personal responsibility for the choices he makes. (But my wife would like to also underscore that he may not become a man at all if he is killed by unforgiving females for leaving the toilet seat up. But this is the LAST editorial comment she gets to make in this chapter.)

A major problem in American society today is a widespread unwillingness to hold ourselves or others responsible for personal choices. This problem is particularly acute in teens, who typically do not face the same "reality check," or sanctions, faced by adults.

EXAMPLE: If you, as an adult, mess up too many times on the job, you will get fired, and this is particularly true if you make stupid excuses for your failures, unless, of course, you are running for president, in which case you will be rewarded with spacious accommodations and the ability to order a launch of cruise missiles, but let's not go there right now.

The point is that most adults who are not world leaders face some limits on their ability to evade responsibility for their actions. But teens seem to be remarkably insulated from the concept of "cause and effect," and in many cases this is because parents treat teens like children instead of young adults.

For much of human history, there was no recognized block of years dubbed "adolescence." A boy was either a child or an adult. And the transformation took place in one day, very often in the form of a ceremony in which the boy was initiated into adulthood by the father and a group of other men.

This event could also be marked by a time alone

in the wilderness, where the young person would fend for himself, or kill a large animal, or do SOME-THING to lay claim to adult status. (HISTORICAL NOTE: In no ancient culture did this ceremony EVER involve Mom and Dad paying for the sharp increase in the automobile insurance premium, so DON'T get your hopes up, young people.)

One day I got a call from my lifelong friend Tim Holler, who decided to do his own initiation cere-mony—sort of a cross between a Christian Bar Mitz-vah and a Boy Scout camp—for his son Seth, who would be turning thirteen in a few short weeks.

Tim was calling just about every male friend and family member possible, requesting that they draft a letter to Seth outlining just what it means to be a man. He received letters from Seth's grandfathers, uncles, adult cousins, and close family friends. Those who lived nearby, or who could take the time to travel, were invited on a camping trip, during which the ini-tiation ceremony would be held.

The Hollers live in Tennessee and we live in Cali-fornia, so I couldn't make the trip out, but Tim reported that the event was deeply moving for Seth and everyone else involved. Tim read the letters around the glow of the fire, and those present offered their own observations about life and manhood.

Seth heard frank admissions of personal failures, warnings about common pitfalls that men face, and encouragement to live a life worthy of the God who made him in His own image. Then Seth the boy was welcomed into the company of men.

Although I could not be there, I did provide Seth with a letter of my own. Distilling my thoughts on manhood down to just a few pages required some serious soul-searching. Ultimately, I elected to focus on the critical issue of personal responsibility. This was the best gift I felt I could offer Seth, who was just a toddler when I helped Tim and his wife, Pam, load up the U-Haul truck and leave the Golden State. I really hadn't been a part of Seth's life, so this was my "window of opportunity" to play a significant role.

The letter appears below, reprinted (with Seth's permission) exactly as he received it back in 1996. I am told that Seth treasures that letter to this very day.

November 17, 1996

Dear Seth,

This will probably reach you late, but it is all the fault of your dad. That is one of the first things you need to learn as you enter male adulthood—it is always someone else's fault. "Find a scapegoat"— that's my motto! This is particularly helpful when the scapegoat can be your dad. I have found him useful for that purpose on many occasions.

Others will try to convince you that as you mature, you need to become more and more responsible and honorable. Not me.

"Why take the rap when Tim is standing right there?"—that's one of my other mottoes.

Let us suppose, for example, that I get a call from your dad a few weeks before your birthday, and he tells me about this neat father/son bonding/training welcome-to-manhood initiation thing he is going to do for you since you are turning 13. And let us suppose that he is collecting letters from key influential males, such as myself. And let us suppose that I agree to send such a letter, giving you wads of wisdom and encouragement that I have amassed over the years like dust bunnies behind a refrigerator that has not been cleaned since Jimmy Carter was President (who was attacked by a REAL bunny! Ask your dad sometime).

And let us suppose that I got kind of busy and just plain forgot. If that were to happen, I could 'fess up (that is Southern talk for "spill the black-eyed peas") that I am late and it is all my fault, thereby teaching you a valuable moral lesson about honesty and personal responsibility.

On the other hand, in keeping with Motto #1, I could also point out that your dad has known for a FULL THIRTEEN YEARS that this date was coming. He could have therefore given me THIR-TEEN years to get ready for this momentous occasion, but he just schlepped along and then suddenly thrust it upon me a mere two weeks out. In fact, I could point out that Tim and I were in the same class in roughly third grade, so he, theoretically, could have asked me about this occasion during the Lyndon Johnson Administration.

So do you think for one moment that I am going to take the heat for this? Not on your South-ern Drawl (which can also be blamed on your dad, who moved you at a very young age from Califor-nia—where we all speak normally and surf every single day—to Memphis, where they invented humidity and insects).

Seth, your life will go so much better if you learn to pin everything on your pappy (that is, once again, Southern talk for "The Big Galoot Who Lives With Your Mom").

Blaming someone else is what being a guy is all about. It all started with Adam, whose response to being caught eating the forbidden fruit was to point out, "Hey, I'm not the one who invented Eve! And it was HER idea! This must be YOUR fault, God!"

The fact that he got tossed out of the Garden of Eden over that incident, and also became mortal and eventually died and plunged the entire human race into moral decay does not detract from the genius of this defense. It merely gives us someone else to blame—Adam!

I hope you find this helpful. If not, don't blame me!

> Cordially,
> Uncle Dave

(You will note that I said Seth still treasures this letter. I made no such assertion about his dad.)

Personal responsibility is an issue that often crops up in our home. We discuss it regularly with Mark and Brad, especially when they do something hurtful to someone else and need to apologize for it. This irritates the daylights out of them, but it is still one of the responsibilities we have as parents (and one of the joys, if our kids are to be believed).

Mark has a tendency to tell his little brother what to do and can be far too critical of Brad over extremely trivial matters. We call him on this when we observe it.

EXAMPLE:

Mark: (*watching Brad play a racing-car game on the Nintendo unit*) "Hey! Slow down on that curve or you'll crash! I've told you a million times."

Brad: "Yes, master. Play your own way, dork."

Colorful fight ensues and Dad rushes into the fray.

Me: "Mark, you started this fight by putting your nose into Brad's game. Apologize to him."

Mark: "I was just helping him to not crash."

Me: "First, it is none of your business how he plays. Second, don't give him advice unless he asks for it. Third, it is a GAME and no one is going to get hurt."

Mark: "I think he plays it wrong just to bug me."

Me: "I think you owe him an apology for starting a fight."

Mark: "He's the one who called me a name!"

Me: "And I am talking to you about what YOU did, not what Brad did. You know you are not supposed to critique his game. We have had this conversation before. So apologize."

Mark: *(to Brad)* "SAR-EEE!"

Me: "Not good enough. You will stand here and practice until you get it right, even if it takes until you have dentures. Say it politely, and also say what you are sorry for."

Mark: *(to Brad)* "I'm sorry I butted into your game and told you what to do."

Brad: "That's OK, dork."

Me: "Ha, ha, ha, ha, ha!"

Mark: "DAD!"

Me: "Oops. It was funny. Brad, now it's your turn to apologize."

Brad: "I figured I would have to, so I just wanted to get one more 'dork' in to make it worth it."

Me:	"Ha, ha, ha, ha, ha!"
Mark:	"DAD!"
Me:	"Brad, apologize."
Brad:	*(to Mark)* "I'm sorry I pointed out you are a dork who is obsessed by how I play my own game."
Mark:	"DAD! This isn't fair!"
Me:	"Brad, just apologize now or the game gets turned off for the rest of the day."
Brad:	"Mark, I'm sorry I called you a name. It was immoral and tragic. A crisis, even."
Me:	"Ha, ha, ha, ha, ha!"
Mark:	"DAD! You are letting him get away with making fun of me!"
Me:	"Brad, to your room. The game is off."

· Brad leaves, giggling.

Me:	"Mark, that whole scene would have not occurred if you hadn't started up with Brad."
Mark:	"I know, and I apologized. Now are you going to apologize to me for laughing at me?"
Me:	"Laughing at you? I wasn't laughing at you. I was laughing at what Brad said."
Mark:	"But he was making fun of me and you were laughing along like it was OK, so it's just like you were laughing at me. I think you owe me an apology."
Me:	"You're right, son. I'm sorry Brad made me crack up at you. But he was so funny I couldn't help it. It isn't my fault."

These kinds of "teachable moments" are invaluable

in conveying to your boys the importance of taking personal responsibility.

And it is vital that you, the parent, model the appropriate behavior because there are hundreds of bad examples out there.

For instance, not to name names or anything, but have you ever noticed how certain politicians will resist apologizing for what they have personally done wrong, but will instead go to preposterously great lengths to apologize for sins they didn't commit?

Let's say that an elected official makes an inappropriate lunge at a female member of his staff, and it somehow gets splashed all over the front page. Does he immediately apologize and repent and seek forgiveness and then vacate his office in disgrace? Not on your executive privilege! And *certainly* not until someone has irrefutable evidence (preferably genetic). He'll deny *everything* as long as humanly possible.

But until there is literally no corner left in which to hide, he will invariably find something ELSE to apologize for in an apparently cynical attempt to throw us, the voters, off guard.

So he will travel to, say, France, or some other country where he has never been accused of inappropriately lunging at anyone, and there, with much pomp and fanfare, he will apologize for the tragedy of the War of 1812, or he'll go to England and apologize that they are terrible cooks, or apologize for ANYTHING that he is in no way personally connected to, such as Scottish Shrubbery Blight.

I call this "Impersonal Responsibility."

Saying "I am deeply sorry about the outbreak of Scottish Shrubbery Blight"—no matter how tragic it may be—has NOTHING to do with personal responsibility (unless the disease is a direct result of your making an inappropriate lunge at a topiary).

But at least we have a tough and skeptical press corps to challenge this transparent ploy.

EXAMPLE:

Press guy: "Mr. Elected Official, with all the allegations swirling around you, how do you expect us to take the Scottish Shrubbery Blight crisis seriously? Unless, of course, you clearly indicate that you are proposing a huge funding increase to combat this scourge?"

Elected Official: "I'm glad you asked, Dan. I am asking Congress to pass an emergency appropriation of $6.2 billion for that very purpose, which underscores just how deeply sorry and apologetic and remorseful I am over this issue."

Press guy: "There you have it, America. Our Elected Official has shown that he is sincere. This was a courageous move and should silence his toady little critics in Congress."

That's why I don't let my kids watch the news.

But, regrettably, bad examples abound even outside of the political realm. Your boys are going to see a lot of irresponsibility over the course of their life. They will see it at school, on the job, and even in the church.

So you, the parent, are going to have do all you can to be a stellar example of integrity and honesty, taking your lumps when you deserve them, and even apologizing to your kids when you blow it with them.

They are not fools. And they are watching you like a **hawk.**

There is no substitute for personal responsibility, especially since Seth and I have already put "dibs" on Tim.

Bummer for you.

Chapter 15

The (Almost) Endless Summer

My wife and I taught a fifth grade Sunday school class, which helps explain our heavy dependence on prescription tranquilizers.

We took this task on as a temporary assignment just for the summer, which, due to the periodic weather phenomenon known as El Ninja, lasted twenty-five months. At least, that's what our church's Christian education pastor, Paul, kept telling us.

"Don't you think summer is about over?" I asked one day as snow blanketed the parking lot.

"Regrettably, no," Paul replied. "This is a particularly nasty El Nino event. I hear it may last another eighteen months. It was just your luck to take on the class during the 'endless summer.'"

"And we don't even get any Beach Boys music out of the deal," I groused.

My wife, Dale, is of the opinion that when it comes to teacher recruitment and retention, the average Christian education pastor adopts the personal integrity of a billiards hustler.

"Paul will use anything to hold on to teachers, including handcuffs," Dale said one day.

"I thought that was a new bracelet," I replied.

"We have to make a break for it," she replied grimly. "I don't buy his El Nitwit explanation for one minute. It's forty-two degrees outside. If this is summer, I'm the duchess of Kansas."

"Kansas doesn't have a duchess," I replied.

"My point exactly," she said.

"Paul said to blame global cooling," I ventured, unwilling to believe that a Christian minister would stoop to fudging the truth.

"Last week I caught him in your office flipping the calendar back two months," she replied. "Mark and Brad are getting edgy about not having birthday parties anymore. If we don't do something soon, we'll be in fifth grade until they wheel us to the nursing home."

It isn't that Dale and I don't believe in shouldering our share of ministry responsibilities. On the contrary, over the years we have done nursery duty, taught youth group, high school Sunday school, adult classes, vacation Bible school, plus a few more. And we have honestly enjoyed it.

But for some reason, teaching fifth grade Sunday school was not so much a ministry as it was a barbarous fight for survival.

To begin with, the class had a high ratio of boys to girls. And these boys were right out of *Lord of the Flies.* They blew spitwads, sat backward, fiddled with lesson papers, wrestled, talked out of turn, and even when, on rare occasions, they were seriously trying to participate, it seemed that something was always just a bit off.

"Does anyone want to share something you are thankful for?" I asked.

Johnny Simmons (not his real name—you'll soon understand why) raised his hand.

"My parents went to Las Vegas last weekend and won 200 bucks."

"Oh. Well. Tell them we are very happy for them," I stammered.

And that's the way it seemed to go all the time, no matter how hard we tried or what we did.

We tried changing the curriculum, holding class outside, sending unruly students out of the room, and issuing stern warnings, but to no avail. One day Paul called me to ask how the class was going.

"Paul, we are dying in there," I said and explained what we were up against.

He listened patiently and then offered an observation and some advice.

"You have an active group of kids. That's normal for fifth graders. But you also have some kids from broken homes, homes with a lot of stress, and other serious problems I can't really go into. A lot of your kids will have trouble focusing. Don't expect them to be good listeners. You'll have to engage them in activities. Wrap the lesson in movement and motion. Use object lessons, like Jesus did. Tell a story. And when you find a teachable moment, kick the lesson as far away as possible and grab the opportunity. You are not there to get through a curriculum; you are there to teach."

Paul can be remarkably wise and understanding as

long as the subject does not involve our not teaching anymore. So I went back with a different approach.

"This is today's object lesson," I said one morning, holding up an Oreo cookie, which instantly got their attention. "The lesson is that you don't get an Oreo at the end of class if you don't sit down and LISTEN and PARTICIPATE and be POLITE."

Some would call it bribery. But it worked, so I call it manna from heaven (just a little darker and rounder version, and with more sugar in the middle).

But I didn't stop at bribery. An Oreo can buy you a moment of quiet, but it does not teach a class.

"How many of you saw at least part of the Olympics on TV?" I asked.

Every hand shot up, which was what I had hoped for. The Olympics had just wrapped up that week.

"Did any of you see the story about the Japanese monks?"

"I DID!" came the simultaneous reply from half of them.

"What did they do every day?"

"They ran practically the whole day," Jeff answered.

"Why?"

"They would do prayers and stuff at all these little temples on the way," said Julie. "That's how they would try to go to heaven. They had to reach every little temple in one day."

I nodded.

"You were really paying attention," I said. "They also had a rope tied around their waist. What was that for?"

Kevin spoke up.

"If they don't run the whole distance in one day, even if they break their leg or something, they have to hang themselves to death!" he said.

"So let me get this straight," I mused aloud. "To get to heaven you have to run a marathon every day, and pray at little temples, and if you fail, you have to commit suicide. Does that sound like what the Bible teaches?"

"NO!" was the unanimous verdict.

"Well, for the rest of this class I am a Japanese monk. If my way isn't the answer, then what is?"

"Jesus died for our sins," said Jeff, but the answer was almost ho-hum. He had been giving the same "right" answer for years.

"Jesus who?" I replied. "I've never heard of him."

"What?" Jeff replied.

"I told you. I am a monk from another land. I hope to find salvation by self-discipline and running more than twenty miles every day and offering prayers at temples. This is the only way I know. If you have a different way, please share it with me. But don't assume I know anything about what you are telling me. You will have to explain it all, and prove it to me as well."

There was a stunned silence.

"Where do we get the answers?" Jeff asked.

"I have no idea," I replied. "But if you are going to say my way is wrong, shouldn't I expect YOU to have the answers?"

We stared at each other for a while.

Then one of the kids shouted, " 'I am the way, the truth and the life! No one comes to the Father but by me!' Jesus said that! So that proves He is the right way!"

"I'm not sure I believe that," I said. "Just because someone says he is the Way doesn't mean it is true. Why should I believe him?"

"Because He is God's Son!" said Mike.

"Prove it," I said.

"He said He was!"

"Talk is cheap."

We stared at each other again. Then Mike lunged for his Bible. A collective light clicked on, and a dozen pairs of little hands grabbed Bibles and began furiously turning pages. Except for Kara.

"This isn't fair," she said. "You're the teacher, so you have to say the answers!"

"I am not your teacher. I am a Japanese monk and you guys said my way is wrong, but you can't prove it. I am not going to abandon everything I believe unless you can give me a very good reason. How will you prove that your Jesus is the Way?"

"Miracles!" replied Jeff. "He fed, like, a ton of people with one piece of bread! And He walked on water!"

"Wow. That catches my interest," I said.

"AND HE ROSE FROM THE DEAD!" Mike shouted.

They had never been so engaged in a lesson. We explored all kinds of verses, many of which they had memorized in prior years but simply had never been put in a position where they actually had to use them. All in all, they did a great job. The monk converted.

In subsequent weeks, we took Paul's advice and blew off the lesson plan on a regular basis, depending on what the kids seemed to respond to. It was a bit unnerving in the sense that we were really winging it a lot of the time, but the class was engaged enough to make it work.

One day I simply wrote on the board, *The question I would most like to ask God is . . .*

The kids wrote their questions, unsigned per my instructions, and we spent the entire class period talking about the issues that they really wanted to know about. The questions ranged from "When did God begin?" to "How will I die, and why?"

I think they were fascinated by the fact that their teachers were taking risks. There were no pat answers out of a lesson plan, because we were making up the lesson as we went along.

There are downsides to this approach. For example, it is hard to be systematic when you are flying by the seat of your pants. And it would be very easy to go off on rabbit trails and never give the kids a fixed "point" to walk away with. You need to be quick thinking and have a reasonably good grasp of the Bible.

But in this case, the excitement of doing something new, and far more challenging, really hooked the kids. And we made a concerted effort to ask hard questions that made them wrack their brains. When we did go back to the prepared lessons, they seemed more focused.

The endless summer finally ended. Coincidentally, it was on the same day Paul found a new teacher.

We breathed an industrial-strength sigh of relief.

I don't regret teaching the class, and, like a lot of guys say, now I can declare, "I'm glad I went through boot camp." It was worth it, but you pay a price.

It was time to let someone else take a crack at it. Dale and I needed something a little easier.

"Paul said he'd like us to try sixth grade when the fall semester starts," I told Dale. "I told him, 'Anything but fifth grade.'"

"Have fun," Dale said.

"What do you mean?" I asked.

"I'm back in choir. You're on your own."

"Well, it will be fine," I said. "Paul assured me that sixth grade is much easier than fifth. That's the only reason I agreed to do it."

Dale looked at me, shaking her head.

"Did you stop to think that the same kids who are in this year's fifth grade class will be in your sixth grade class in the fall?" she asked. "Did he offer to sell you the Brooklyn Bridge, too?"

Christian education pastors are the reason God gave us Prozac.

Chapter 16

The Normally Abnormal Home

All little boys operate on the frighteningly inaccurate premise that "normal" is defined by whatever happens in their homes. This is true whether the kids belong to a U.S. senator or the school custodian, the main difference being that the custodian's kids do not typically learn to expect vicious thirty-second television commercials about their father (unless the teachers are trying to send him a *very* strong message about the cleanliness of the faculty lounge).

One day when Mark was about three, he was playing at the home of a little friend named Michelle, who was an only child at that time. Bradley, whom Mark referred to as "Datley," was hanging out in the playpen alone doing the drool thing. Later that day Mark asked, "Why doesn't Michelle have a Datley?"

Based on his experience, limited though it was, he expected every other kid to have a little drool-o-matic playmate known as a "Datley."

I explained that some kids had no Datleys, while others had lots of Datleys.

His eyes widened as he rapidly assimilated the following new information:

—Other families are different from ours!

—Some kids don't even have a Datley!

—But other kids have *more* Datleys than me!

—***Hey, I'm getting gypped out of Datleys!***

"I wouldn't like not having a Datley," he said.

"Me neither," I replied.

"Can I have some more Datleys?" he wondered.

Shamelessly taking advantage of his short attention span, I suggested we go look at some puppies.

I remember that incident because it crystallized for me just how my son viewed reality. Whatever happened in our family was considered by Mark to be the norm against which the rest of the world was judged. Even the way Dale made a sandwich was the "right" way, and other moms' sandwiches were critiqued by how closely they replicated her ideal sandwich.

My mind raced back to my own childhood, and similar thought processes—and I use that term generously—I had when I was young.

My father smoked when I was a kid, but my mother did not. It therefore did not faze me to see other dads smoke. But I almost fell off my chair the first time I ever saw a woman smoke.

I was SHOCKED.

I was STUNNED.

I could NOT believe my eyes.

Smoking was just *not* something women did, because, well, *my* mom didn't.

I had a similar reaction one day in the grocery store when I was shopping with my mom and we bumped into my kindergarten teacher.

I was SHOCKED.

I was STUNNED.

I could NOT believe my eyes.

What was my teacher doing in a STORE instead of our class?

I was speechless.

My mom thought I was being rude, but I wasn't. I said nothing as they chatted, but the minute we changed aisles I blurted out, "What is Mrs. Marshall doing here?"

Mom looked at me, puzzled. "What do you mean?"

"Why isn't she at school?" I asked.

Mom laughed.

"Even teachers have to shop," Mom said. "They don't live at the school."

I gasped.

"They DON'T?????"

She might just as well have said that the chalkboards were shipped to China every night and whisked back to class just before the bell rang.

A child's profoundly limited view of the world does change over time, of course, but even as kids get older they will largely continue, consciously or unconsciously, to judge normality against their own experience at home. Kids are enormously impressionable.

If dad "A" gets plastered on the weekend to "unwind," that is going to define for his kids just what it means to unwind. Dad "A" should not be surprised if his kids develop an alcohol problem.

Conversely, if dad "B" helps build houses for Habitat for Humanity during his time off, that kind of volunteer service will likewise be seen as a normal part of adult life. His kids are apt to value helping their fellow man.

If dad "C" listens to polka music, his boys will think he is a geek and move into the Habitat for Humanity house. Hey, I only said they were impressionable, not tone deaf.

The salient point here is that for good or ill, you, the parent, are establishing the framework for your child's worldview, character development, and choices.

This is not to say that a child's future is inevitably determined by his homelife. There are kids who grow up in very rocky home situations with very poor role models who nevertheless turn out to be really neat people. We cannot discount the grace of God.

And there are kids who had great parents and a nurturing home but nevertheless choose to embrace a very sinful lifestyle. Human beings have the freedom to make choices, including bad choices. We cannot discount the powerful pull of sin.

But both common sense and empirical evidence tell us that—generally speaking—loving and moral homes are far more likely to beget loving and moral kids than awful and immoral homes. Kids tend to imitate the attitudes and actions modeled by their parents.

Probably the stupidest comment a parent can make to his kid is "Do as I say, not as I do."

Kids *WILL* do as you do, particularly when they are younger, *because whatever you do defines normality*.

This helps explain why many children will accept absolutely awful levels of physical and emotional abuse before someone finally comes to their rescue. They didn't realize it was abuse—they thought it was just normal life.

Not meaning to throw a wet blanket on anyone's celebration of diversity or anything, but go scan some old *National Geographic* magazines sometime and observe the truly wacko stunts that are pulled in obscure little nations. You'll see photos of kids in the middle of a multiyear process of reshaping their lower lip until it is the approximate size and shape of a small pizza. They didn't think this up on their own. Their dad has a lower lip the size of a Volkswagen.

Closer to home, I seriously doubt that any group of kids would spontaneously decide to invent a new fad consisting of drying some tobacco leaves, wrapping them in paper, sticking them in their mouths, setting them on fire, and then barfing. I have a hunch that they are imitating adult behavior.

Until they gain some maturity, most kids just assume that whatever happens in their home happens in every home. This is the case whether Mom and Dad respect each other or despise each other.

I remember Mark coming home from his first day at a new school. As he was getting to know another kid, he was asked, "Who do you live with?"

That question was casually lumped in with all the other questions ranging from "What's your name?" to "What did you bring for lunch?"

Mark had no idea what "Who do you live with?" meant.

"Uh, my parents and my brother, and my dog," he said.

"Who gets you the most?"

"Huh?" answered Mark.

"Who do you stay with the most?"

"What?" inquired Mark, completely confused.

"Do you live mostly at your mom's house or your dad's house?" came the exasperated reply.

"We only have one house," Mark replied, still bewildered. "Why would we have two houses?"

"Both of your parents live in the same house?" came the equally bewildered response.

These two boys had such completely different home experiences that they could not immediately relate to each other.

But as children mature, they begin to observe the differences in various homes. They will then often start to pick out new standards of "normal" based upon what they like about other homes. I call this "smorgasbord normality."

This has certainly been true with Mark and Brad, whose definition of "normal" evolved into "whatever is the *opposite* of our home."

As they have gotten older, our boys have chafed at our family standards. Mark and Brad think Dale and I are WAY too uptight and strict and old-fashioned and out of it and . . . you get the general drift.

One day Brad was griping, yet again, about how deprived he is.

"Scott gets to see any movie he wants and he gets to watch as much TV as he wants and no one makes him do his homework. And Jeff can stay up as late as he wants and his dad buys him TONS of stuff."

I knew the punch line was coming.

"How come we can't just be like normal families?" Brad whined.

"You're right," I said.

That stopped him in his tracks.

"I'll tell you what," I continued. "How about if me and Mom try to be like Scott's parents. We'll split up, and I'll move away and you'll almost never see me, and Mom will marry someone else and become totally involved in her own life and ignore you while you fail all your classes and stay glued to the TV."

Brad's mouth dropped open.

"And I'll be like Jeff's dad, too," I said. "I'll basically ignore you except for a few weeks during the summer, but I'll try to buy you off by getting you a bunch of stuff. Sound like a deal?"

"That isn't what I mean," Brad said, dropping the whine and turning serious.

"Do you think Scott and Jeff are happy with what has happened to their families?" I asked.

"No. It makes them sad, but they don't really talk about it. But it makes Scott really mad when his dad says he will visit and he waits all day and it doesn't happen. He hates his dad."

We talked all afternoon. Deep down, Brad was very grateful that Dale and I had never even hinted at splitting up. He saw the scars borne by his friends. Our "boring" life is, at least, stable and safe.

But he was still dazzled by all the glitz and "freedom" that marked the lives of his friends.

"Why can't we have both?" he finally asked. "Why can't you and Mom love each other, and love me and Mark, but give us more freedom and more stuff? I just want a normal life."

"Brad, 'normal' is a hard thing to pin down," I said. "Mom and I are not rich, and there is no way we can buy all the stuff Jeff's dad buys him. And we wouldn't even if we could. Having stuff is not what life is all about.

"But we have tried to let you *do* a lot of neat stuff—like the trip across the country. You got to go inside the St. Louis Arch, see the Grand Canyon, watch fireworks over the Mississippi River, and even touch the famous Statue of the Enraged Colorado Woodchuck. How many of your friends have done that?"

"I don't remember any woodchuck," replied Brad.

"Just making sure you aren't tuning me out," I said.

"Well, all that was cool, but what I really want is more TV and movies," he replied.

"Mom and I are not going to let you waste your mind on more TV, and we are not going to have you watch movies that we think are inappropriate and damaging.

"We do want you to have a normal life, but we are not going to define normal based on what the popular culture is doing at any given point. Popular culture has produced all kinds of bad and dangerous stuff, including bell-bottoms and disco music. We are going to try as hard as we can to let God define what is normal and live that way."

That talk did not end our conflict over what constitutes a normal life. But it did help us understand each other better. And indeed, there is room for movement on both sides.

Although Dale and I often disagree with Mark and Brad over what a "normal life" really is, we all can agree on what is abnormal: strife, hostility, angry words, threats.

On the other hand, the "fruit of the Spirit" seems like a wonderful definition of a normal home: love, joy, peace, patience, gentleness, goodness, self-control.

Of course, the kids are quick to point out that nothing in that list seems to sanction our dumping the Ice Cubes of Happiness in their beds when they fail to get up on time. But we point out that nothing in that list requires us to keep paying them for doing chores.

Stalemate.

I have come to the conclusion that it is normal for kids to start out thinking that whatever Mom and Dad do is normal, but later conclude that everything Mom and Dad do is abnormal, and then ultimately come back to Mom and Dad's point of view once they have kids of their own. Unless that parental point of view includes polka music.

Chapter 17

School and Your Boys

—or—

Time Travel in the Third Grade

"I would like to explain why I changed Brad's seating assignment," explained the teacher as Dale and I listened in embarrassment during Back-to-School Night.

When humiliation kicks in I begin to fade out, so I missed most of the details. But I do recall snippets of the conversation.

"Cutting up . . . jokes with Daniel . . . needs to focus . . . genuinely nice boy . . . but the incident with the whoopee cushion . . . a talk with him."

I could see Dale's mind whirring. First, Brad would be grounded. Second, he would lose his allowance. Third, he would eat gruel in his cell for the next ten years.

My entire elementary school education flashed before my eyes as Brad's teacher outlined my son's offenses. I shuddered at the memory of a particular incident that took place decades earlier when I was Brad's age. . . .

I was in the third grade long before the feminist

movement really got rolling, which partly explains why Miss Brinkley did not think twice about having each of her pupils engage in the now unthinkable act of standing up on the first day of class to "share what your **daddy does** for a living."

In those days, the teacher felt she could safely assume that (1) each of our homes had a daddy rather than a Significant Male; (2) because none of our mothers were fellow teachers she already knew what they did for a living; and (3) her twenty-five students actually had some notion as to where their fathers went to toil every day.

Two out of three wasn't bad. And misjudging number three can be explained by the fact that (1) this was her first day of teaching; (2) she had therefore never given this particular activity its ritual "first and last" try; and (3) the education spirits, who are far less merciful than any ancient Aztec deity, decreed that the unmarried young maiden must undergo the initiation by fire—teaching third grade at Lincoln Street School.

She scanned the room for an eager face and incorrectly assumed that because Darrell Bakersfield was bobbing vigorously up and down in his seat he wanted to go first. Those of us who had endured the previous three grades with Darrell, however, correctly assumed that we had better take cover as quick as we could. Whenever Darrell got nervous in class (and calling on him did nothing if not make him nervous), he began to quake like a volcano shortly before he erupted like one.

"BARF ATTACK!" yelled Billy Hampton as two dozen battle-scarred third graders unhesitatingly adopted civil-defense positions under their desks while fifth-grader-sized Mike Coughlan seized the ticking bomb and whisked it to the boys' room where it could safely be detonated.

"All clear," Billy announced a moment later. "You may return to your seats. Miss Brinkley, the class is again yours."

A barf attack is a rough way to break in a new teacher, but she came through with flying colors— beginning with turning stark white as shock drained the blood from her face, then growing to a deeply flustered red as she climbed out from under her desk, and then transforming back to a kind of blotchy pink as she again took command of her class.

"It seems that you all understand and have adapted to Darrell's apparent, um, condition," she said as she wiped the beads of perspiration from her brow. "I commend you for it."

Apparently undaunted by her narrow escape, she again surveyed the room for an eager or, at minimum, un-nauseated face. It is my curse to have never mastered the sick, plaintive grimace that is to a teacher what quills are to a predatory animal: the unspoken warning "Not me."

"David, would you like to go first?" she asked.

We did not learn the term "rhetorical question" until years later in freshman literature and composition, but we nevertheless learned in kindergarten that "Would you like to go first?" had only one correct answer unless you wanted to go home with a sealed note requesting that you be smacked into the middle of next week.

Actually, since none of us had the courage to risk death by opening a teacher's sealed note, we could only surmise the contents of the envelope by a scientific cataloging of parental responses to the top-secret directive.

We were divided into roughly two schools of thought, one of which adhered to the "Smack Him Into the Middle of Next Week" hypothesis (with sixty percent of the vote), and the other group accepting the "Take Away All His Toys for a Week" theory (with thirty-two percent). The other eight percent constituted inexplicable responses ranging from a quiet, concerned chat about "needing to improve your class participation" (Johnny Schmitz got this one, accompanied by a trip downtown for a milk shake with his dad!) to being grounded for life. So we simply lumped those aberrations together in the "other" category.

Since I belonged to the majority school of thought, I made a quick and wise decision to answer the rhetorical question in the affirmative. Having made such a commitment, however, I suddenly faced the not insignificant obstacle of explaining my father's career while in fact having no earthly idea how he fed and clothed our family.

While he had discussed his job in general terms like "that stinking hole" or "that two-bit Mickey Mouse outfit," I could not recall any specifics.

I stood up, bit one side of my lip, cleared my throat, put my hands in my pockets, bit the other half of my lip, took my hands back out of my pockets, and cleared my throat again, but my brain was blank. The thought flashed through my mind that I could simply admit the truth and sit down, but I was too embarrassed. A kid should know what his pop does for a living.

"Punt before you puke," whispered Billy, a piece of advice he had often given, without much effect, to Darrell.

So I punted.

"My dad is a scientist," I announced, then sat down as a wave of relief swept over me.

"How interesting!" exclaimed Miss Brinkley. "Please, don't sit down yet. Tell us more about his work."

Recklessly disregarding a recent Supreme Court ruling on the subject, I silently launched into a quick and earnest prayer right there on school grounds.

"You're dead," Billy whispered helpfully.

But Billy was a mere Methodist and therefore lacked my advantage with heaven. Growing up Catholic, I could invoke dozens of saints, all of whom had lots of free time on their hands and all of whom were aware that I had not yet undergone Holy Confirmation so patron-saint status was up for grabs to whoever would help me within the next five seconds. I chose Saint Jude—an almost unconscious decision that was most likely prompted by the thought that I might soon be in a hospital that bore his name.

In a blinding flash of insight, the answer came.

"Time travel," I said with the confidence of a prophet, my gaze fixed firmly heavenward. "He works in time travel."

My heavenward gaze did not preclude a quick glance at my classmates. About 60 percent of them experienced a quick, involuntary shudder as they reflected on my upcoming fate, 32 percent began whispering that I would never see my bike again, and the remaining 8 percent bolted from the room in the form of Mike Coughlan rushing Darrell to the boys' room again.

(It wasn't that Mike enjoyed danger, or that he was especially bighearted, that made him volunteer to risk total grodiness for Darrell's sake. It was because, having been grounded for life after he feigned, with entirely convincing sincerity, during a field trip to the zoo that Timmy Smith had fallen into the tiger pit, he grasped at any opportunity to bolt from restrictive spaces.)

Miss Brinkley was staring at me rather sternly.

"David, that is very amusing," she said unamusedly. "But we are not here to engage in silliness. Now, tell us what your father does or I will have to send you home with a note."

I sensed that it would not be the note urging a concerned chat and a milk shake.

"But he really has worked on time travel," I insisted, explaining how just last month when I had categorically proven that it is entirely possible to set a shed on fire using nothing more than fireworks, my dad (in a show of scientific competitiveness) sought to outdo my feat by attempting to launch me into the middle of the next week.

"Even though he only got me as far as the following Tuesday, it worked in principle," I explained.

Apparently impressed by his preliminary work, Miss Brinkley wrote Dad a congratulatory note (sealed), which must have encouraged him to press on to success. He not only propelled me to the middle of the next week, he actually managed to land me in another month.

"Thank you," Dale said to the teacher, nudging me to follow suit.

I was suddenly snapped back to the present like a spaceship making the jump to light speed.

"Thank you, yes," I stammered. "We'll make sure he stops, uh, whatever it is he isn't supposed to keep doing. Right away. Certainly by the middle of next week. Did anyone barf?"

Dale extracted us from the classroom before I made a further idiot out of myself.

"Dave, what is wrong with you?" she asked. "You acted like you were on a different planet during that entire meeting."

"Time warp," I replied.

"What?"

"Don't worry," I said.

"So what are we going to do about Brad?" she asked.

"Let he who is without sin among you cast the first stone. Jesus said that, you know," I countered.

"What is wrong with you?" she asked again. "And, again, what are we going to do about Brad?"

I stroked my chin and pondered for a moment.

"First, I'll take him downtown for a milk shake. Then, we will have a concerned chat," I said.

"How is that a punishment?"

"I've always wanted to find out," I replied.

Chapter 18

When Angels Fly Airplanes

The book of Hebrews instructs us to "not neglect hospitality to strangers, for by doing so some have entertained angels without knowing it." (However, Bible commentators across all denominational lines agree that if a stranger arrives at your door and mentions the phrase "whole life policy," this is a sure sign he is not from heaven and you don't have to go through the bother of killing the fatted calf or even necessarily serving pretzels.)

But that directive to show hospitality is a real challenge for me, as I am not a particularly social person by nature. I am polite when meeting new people, but I typically have just a couple of truly close friends.

My wife, Dale, on the other hand, can literally meet someone for the first time and chat for just a few minutes and then be perfectly comfortable inviting them over for dinner and a lengthy and meaningful conversation that lasts for hours. She is *thrilled* to entertain others in our home, and she does not feel the least bit gypped if they don't turn out to be angels.

They don't even have to be Methodists.

I am actually amazed at just how hospitable she can be, but I will also admit that sometimes my attitude about graciousness is not nearly as Christian as it ought to be. Left to myself, I could probably rationalize "hospitality" down to cutting a check to the Salvation Army once a year. Dale is the main reason we have friends at all.

This character flaw of mine rose to the surface one day when Dale asked me if I was OK with the idea of having strangers over for Thanksgiving.

"Not really," I answered. "I'd just like to spend it with family. I don't want to feel like I have to make conversation all afternoon with people I don't know."

"It's a good thing you weren't one of the Indians who met the first Pilgrims, or our forefathers would have all starved to death," she said.

Dale has always been subtle when making a point.

"Who are you going to invite?" I sighed, resigning myself to the inevitable.

"My sister's husband's brother and his family," she replied. "You'll love it. I promise. Thanksgiving is a time for sharing."

As it turned out, the day went very well. Art and Sony (rhymes with "Bonnie") were a very nice, down-to-earth couple, and Mark and Brad got along wonderfully with their two boys, Elias and Jeremiah. Art is a pilot and had flown his family into the local airport. He gave everyone a scenic flight, we played games, and generally had a great time. In fact, we invited them back again for other holidays.

Mark and Brad hit it off so well with Jeremiah that one week we had his parents fly him in so he could stay with us for a few days during the summer. Those days deeply affected our home.

Jeremiah is a couple of years older than Mark, my oldest son. So the kids already looked up to him because of his age. But add in the fact that Jeremiah is handsome, muscular, a fantastic artist, a nice guy, and very funny, and you quickly see that the stage is set for some serious hero-worship.

I found that Mark and Brad were trying to outdo each other in proving how cool they could be in his presence, and that effort began to take the form of smarting off to their Mom.

Jeremiah cut that off at the knees.

"Hey, you shouldn't show disrespect to your parents," he said, *very* seriously.

They looked at him in shock.

"Disrespecting your parents is like disrespecting God," he continued. "Don't do it."

The smart-aleck comments ceased at once, and they went outside to play on the trampoline while Dale performed CPR to restart the blood flow to my brain, which had seized up due to shock.

"Did you HEAR that?" I exclaimed when I came to.

Dale was smiling broadly. "I know! It's amazing," she said.

I seized the phone and dialed his mother.

"Hi, Sony. Hey, everything is going fine. Listen, you aren't interested in selling your son, are you? No? What about a yearly lease with an option to renew? Then just a week-to-week rental agreement. No? You drive a hard bargain. Let's talk cloning, and we'll pay for the mad scientist."

Listen, a cool, athletic, artistic teenager who is committed to Jesus and teaches other kids to respect their parents is worth the entire contents of Buckingham Palace (as long as you leave out Prince Charles). I would have kidnapped him were it not for the fact that—and my wife is *so* legalistic about this—it is a felony.

But the story gets better.

Sunday morning came, and Jeremiah was *eager* to go to church. He looks *forward* to Sunday mornings.

So he is sitting in the pew next to Mark and Brad as the collection plate is being passed and, without fanfare, he drops in thirty dollars. I did not witness this, but my boys surely did. It took an ophthalmologist two hours to replace their eyeballs, which had spontaneously bulged out of their sockets upon witnessing this quiet demonstration of financial sacrifice.

Dale and I overheard our boys peppering Saint Jeremiah with questions on the way home.

"Why did you give all that money?"

"Well, I got paid on Friday. I would usually give at my own church, but since I am staying with you guys, I thought I would just give it while I'm here. It's still for God, no matter where I am."

"But why that MUCH?" asked Brad.

"Well, that's 10 percent of what I made," he replied.

We got home and I lunged again for the phone.

"Sony, you gotta sell. Name your price. You can have another kid. Think of it like getting a new car. You can have a brand-new one and we'll buy your used model."

It was no use. The woman was completely irrational. I even offered to buy her a new crib and fashionable "stretchable" maternity pants and she still wouldn't budge.

The day finally came when it was time for Jeremiah to go back home. Tears were flowing freely by the time we reached the airport.

"Get a grip, Dad!" snapped Mark. "It isn't like you'll never see him again."

Life got back to normal soon enough, but not completely normal.

I was backing the car out of the driveway the following Sunday morning as we prepared to head to church when Mark shouted, "OH NO! I forgot my money!"

"For what?" I replied. "What do you have to buy?"

"It isn't to buy, it's to give," Mark said. "Remember we had that garage sale this week? I made twenty dollars. I need to give 10 percent!"

And thus was the concept of giving to God internalized for Mark. Not because of a sermon, or a lecture from me, or even because of the parental example of giving. It came about because Dale decided, years earlier, to invite some strangers over for Thanksgiving dinner. Otherwise, it is unlikely that we would have ever even met Jeremiah.

"Do not neglect hospitality to strangers, for by doing so some have entertained angels without knowing it."

Now, it isn't like I believe that Jeremiah is an angel or anything, but—hey!—come to think of it, he actually did *fly* into our town.

Hmmmmmm . . .

Chapter 19

Dadipulation

One day Brad walked up to me and held the following note in front of my face:

> Dear loving, kind, caring, sharing, nice, sweet, tender, smart, unselfish Daddy,
>
> **If you love me prove it to me** by (please, please, please, please, please, please) driving me to buy my own Blizzard (I said I would buy my own, with my own money) at Dairy Queen (or DQ). I want you to because I did a ton of hard, breathtaking, heaving jobs (I did), like taking down the Christmas tree lights and cleaning the pool and sawing trees and putting "um" in the humungous burning pile. I practically broke my back by carrying and sawing, so I need something to cool my soul like a cold refreshing chocolate chip cookie dough Blizzard!
>
> Sincerely, your nice, sweet
> Bradley
>
> P.S. If you love me, consider taking me to DQ.

Talk about a cute but nevertheless brazen attempt at manipulation by a ten-year-old. Dinner was almost ready, so his timing could not have been worse. So I took him straight down to Dairy Queen anyway and paid for the milk shake myself.

Dale seeks to cultivate qualities like delayed gratification and dietary roughage, while I balance her out by emphasizing impulse purchases and Captain Crunch cereal.

I think we approach our boys differently, in part, because men are generally WAY less mature than women. Basically, all men are ten-year-olds who are trapped in adult bodies. We may seem mature, but it is only because we have facial hair and deep voices and pretty much run the Senate.

We try to go along with the way our wives want to raise our boys, but deep down inside we, too, wonder how come we can't play first and do our chores later and have ice cream for breakfast when, hey, it is a milk product pretty much just like the stuff we pour on our cereal, just a little colder and with more chocolate syrup and nuts.

Despite all the pathetic rhetoric ever emitted by the National Organization for Women, there are deep and profound differences between men and women, and those differences go WAY beyond who has to take Midol.

I GUARANTEE you that I know which gender will gleefully show their sons how to mash their face against the XEROX machine to make copies of humorous facial expressions. And this particular gender would very likely do this for HOURS were it not for the fact that the glass gets hot and it starts to burn your skin.

Um, not that I know this from personal experience or anything, as I am a mature and responsible professional who wears a tie and has a business card. So I am just conjecturing that after about six copies you need to let the machine rest for about three minutes and then you can shoot another half dozen prints.

But there is another gender that would never even THINK of doing this, even if they were locked in a room for a month with nothing more than dry toast and water and a copying machine. And when this other gender finds the photocopies that you and your sons bring home, they will roll their eyes and just shake their head and be *amazed* that you would find this amusing.

But we DON'T find it amusing. We find it an absolute shrieking HOOT (which is about twelve notches higher than mere amusement). So we see that men are even less mature than women think we are. The guy gender manages to compensate by periodically doing something mature and noble, like writing the Gettysburg Address or inventing the printing press or finding a cure for smallpox or becoming a missionary. But we can lapse back into ten-year-old mode at speeds approaching 186,000 miles per second.

EXAMPLE: Dale and I are friends with a couple named Maggie and Ed, who are both schoolteachers. Ed is a truly deep thinker, and it is not at all rare for him and me to talk for hours at a time about economics, church history, or the philosophical basis of our nation's political institutions. We *enjoy* discussing the economic theories of Adam Smith. Really! Dale and Maggie think we are incredibly sophisticated and thoughtful and dull, so they often have their own conversations about art and gardening and human relationships while Ed and I debate libertarianism.

We were recently involved in just such a conversation when Ed overheard Dale and Maggie chatting in the kitchen.

Me: "That is an unworkable view on foreign policy, Ed. As the world's superpower, we have an enduring obligation in the Middle East."

Dale: *(to Maggie)* ". . . so I could either just throw this old barbecue away, or possibly turn it into a planter with gardenias and set it out in the garden . . ."

Ed: *(to me)* "But as a free people, I think we have the right and responsibility to determine if the immediate security of the nation is . . . Hey, did your wife just say you are thinking of getting rid of the barbecue?"

Me: "I think so."

Ed: "Man, I have some shotgun ammo that we could REALLY have some fun with. These are solid lead slugs that could stop a charging rhino dead in its tracks."

Me: "Wow! We could blow that thing to smithereens!"

Ed: "Can you imagine the SOUND?"

Me: "We could put that baby into ORBIT!"

Ed: "I think we could basically vaporize it, especially if we seal the holes and fill it with water!"

Me: "Why don't we get Mark and Brad and . . ."

We then notice that Dale and Maggie are staring at us in dead silence. They roll their eyes and sigh and go outside to talk about gardening as a metaphor for interpersonal relationships while Ed and I (and bear in mind that both of us sometimes lead adult Bible studies) continue to discuss blowing the barbecue to Lithuania.

Men are made out of the same genetic material as their sons (a complex DNA strain that includes a high quotient of Chips-Ahoy molecules). Because of this genetic similarity, we act like our kids. So naturally, a father's sympathy is easily aroused by his sons—and they use it to great effect to manipulate Dad.

My kids have even stooped to pulling down on their cheeks so that they resemble basset hounds, and then they make whimpering little puppy noises. It gets to me. I hand them cash and pat them on the head while Dale cringes. She believes in earning set amounts of money for doing specific jobs so that our boys will learn that there is a direct cause and effect that links work and rewards. And she also believes in eating appropriate meals, which often include steamed vegetables.

And bran.

Intellectually, I know she is right. And I really do *try* to be supportive, because I know it is important for Dale and me to present a united front. It's just hard because mature thinking and deliberative planning come naturally to her, while I have to keep persuading myself to act my age. So Dale is reinforcing the value of hard work and fiscal prudence, while I am inwardly agreeing with Brad, who has just pointed out that if we run out and charge a boat on my VISA card we can water ski RIGHT NOW while it is still hot outside.

Dale takes to responsibility like a duck to water. I take to responsibility like a duck to a roomful of cougars. It is not a pretty sight.

Because Dale deeply loves our boys and wants what is best for them in the long term, she views her major parental decisions in the light of:

1. How will this affect the boys over the next decade, and
2. How will this factor in their relationship to their future spouses?

I love our kids just as much as she does, but I employ the following decision-making process, which differs somewhat from hers:

1. Is this expressly forbidden in either the Bible or the Code of Federal Regulations, and
2. Would it be fun?

So of course my boys target me when they want something. There is a good reason that linguists coined the word "*Man*ipulation" instead of "*Mom*ipulation."

Fortunately, I am rational enough to at least talk everything over with Dale. I am aware that I may not be able to see that my sons are manipulating my tendency to think like a ten-year-old, so I rely on her judgment like a pilot relies on his instruments, no matter WHAT his feelings say.

EXAMPLE: Brad comes up to me and asks if we can have some family bonding time. He outlines his plan, and it sounds really good to me. Besides, the whole issue of family bonding is something that Dale and I have tried to emphasize, especially as the boys get older. His request seems consistent with our parental goals, and, in fact, seems remarkably mature.

Until Dale gives me "the look."

Dale: "Dave, just because Brad tosses out the
          phrase 'family bonding time,' it does NOT
          mean we can fly to Hawaii next week to go
          surfing."

Me: "But it isn't illegal, and it would be fun."

Dale: "It is also fun to pay the mortgage and eat."

Me: "I suppose skydiving is out as well?"

Dale: "How about a game night right here in
          sunny California in our own home?"

Me: "Do you think Brad really wants some qual-
          ity family time, or was he just trying to
          manipulate my emotions to get what he
          wants?"

Dale: "I really need an aspirin."

So we stayed home and played a game called
"Hangman."

I stared at the sheet of paper my boys handed me
and wracked my brain. It looked like this (the paper, I
mean):

—— —— ——— —— ———— ————
—— ————————— ———.

Hangman is a game where you try to guess the
mystery word by picking out letters one at a time
while the person who knows the word fills in the
blanks each time you guess a correct letter. But this
one was so long it was more like guessing a mystery
novel than a mystery word.

"Come on, just guess!" Mark said.

Every Hangman expert knows that "E" is a fairly

safe entry. So I picked that one.

"That wasn't so hard, was it?" asked Brad, filling in the spaces.

He was right. I hit pay dirt five times. So then it looked like this:

___ __<u>e</u> __ ___<u>e</u> __<u>e</u>_

_<u>e</u> _____ <u>e</u> ___ .

I slowly plodded my way through the puzzle, missing some letters and getting others right. I was so engrossed that I scarcely noticed how the boys edged slowly toward the door each time I guessed a correct letter.

It took ten minutes before I uncovered the secret message:

<u>Y</u> <u>o</u> <u>u</u>   <u>a</u> <u>r</u> <u>e</u>   <u>s</u> <u>o</u>   <u>c</u> <u>u</u> <u>t</u> <u>e</u>   <u>w</u> <u>h</u> <u>e</u> <u>n</u>

<u>w</u> <u>e</u>   <u>m</u> <u>a</u> <u>n</u> <u>i</u> <u>p</u> <u>u</u> <u>l</u> <u>a</u> <u>t</u> <u>e</u>   <u>y</u> <u>o</u> <u>u</u> .

I bolted after them as they ran down the street cackling like adolescent, acne-prone hyenas being chased by an enraged water buffalo with a receding hairline.

But it would not be accurate or fair to imply that boys are the only creatures who engage in manipulation (it's just that they are so blatant about it, they stand out like an airport beacon).

All of us have the temptation to manipulate others to get what we want. Husbands and wives can do this to each other, siblings do it as well, and even employers and employees engage in this dance.

Manipulation is a character flaw because it is a substitute for honesty. It is eventually a detriment to any relationship. It is immature.

We should expect this kind of immaturity in kids, but we should also seek to help them grow beyond it. (Drooling is also a normal and accepted part of being a little kid, but we certainly don't want to see teenagers doing it.)

While Brad's milk shake note was very funny, it contained a theme—*"If you love me, prove it to me by . . . (giving me something)"*—that Dale and I keep working, gently, to correct.

The "something" itself is not the issue. The issue is that relationships have been ruined over the challenge inherent in the phrase "if you love me, prove it by":

getting me the car of my dreams.
taking me on the vacation of my dreams.
buying me the (fill in the blank).
Prove it, prove it, prove it!

The quality of the relationship is the true measure of love. Objects, gifts, and other such stuff are not love, nor do they prove love.

Love gives itself. Love can exist in financial poverty. It is in no way dependent on *stuff*. Sure, love can and often does prompt a tangible expression, such as a gift (or a milk shake). But love is not an exercise in bartering.

I bought Brad a milk shake that day *because* I love him, not to *prove* I love him. He may not have discerned the difference at the time, but that's OK right now. As he grows, I think he will understand.

But what neither the boys nor I will ever fully grasp—because it remains shrouded in mystery—is why, even if we put bran on it, we can't have ice cream for breakfast.

Some mysteries are just too great to comprehend in this life.

Chapter 20

Showers of Blessing
(Yeah, Right)

The cameras always capture the moment so vividly.

The tensed stadium crowd holding its collective breath and then erupting at the same moment. The exultant coach throwing both hands into the air and shouting, "YES!" The close-up of the mom and dad leaping up and down in the stands, choked with emotion as their child breaks a record or wins a coveted gold medal.

Millions of viewing parents all around the globe vicariously experience that rush of emotions.

But for Dale and me, one extraordinary day it did *not* have to be a surrogate excitement viewed on a television screen. It was our very own "one moment in time." And we will never forget it.

At precisely 11:34 P.M. on May 15, 1998, our son Mark, at the tender age of fifteen, set a new world record for the longest continuous period of recorded time a teenager has ever occupied the bathroom.

Dale and I reacted with the deep emotion that any

set of parents would feel at such an historic moment.

"GET OUT OF THERE RIGHT THIS INSTANT!" I yelled, beating on the door.

"There are other people waiting to use the bathroom!" Dale shouted, desperately trying to be heard above the noise of the shower.

"I'm almost finished," Mark called back from behind the locked door.

"That's what you said TWO HOURS ago," Dale snapped, punishing the doorknob with a savage shaking. "GET OUT!"

Much like an Olympic athlete, Mark had spent thousands of grueling hours working up to this shining moment of glory. He was not about to let trifling little impediments—such as parental bladders—stand in the way of destiny.

My mind raced back to the day, thirty-six months earlier, when our Realtor, Patti, showed us the house (and the bathroom) for the first time. Dale and I could not believe our good fortune.

Up to that moment, we had been searching for weeks for a decent house in our price range that contained the amenities we really felt we needed, and we were discouraged. There were plenty of homes we could choose from if we were willing to bend on a few luxuries, such as a functional roof, but everything we had seen was either too tiny, or poorly designed, or on too small a lot, or in need of too much work. But then Patti showed us this one.

It had been on the market for months and no one had even made an offer. It was a 1950s vintage ranch-style house with hardwood floors, three bedrooms plus a den, a great kitchen, a fireplace, a pool, and a massive backyard with fruit trees and grapevines and a shaded deck.

The owners were getting desperate and were willing to work with us on the price. We really liked everything about it, and it was far less expensive than houses that were much smaller and without nearly the features or charm of this older home.

"Why do you think it hasn't sold?" I asked Patti. "Is there some glaring problem we have overlooked? Something hidden, like termites or bad wiring or a secret room containing Roseanne Arnold?"

Patti shook her head. "I honestly think it comes down to one thing," she said. "I agree that the home is very nice, and, in fact, it would be undervalued except for one thing—it only has one bathroom, and most people are just not willing to live with a single bathroom."

Dale and I quickly talked it over and concluded that the combination of price, huge lot, unique architectural features, and newly remodeled kitchen outweighed the disadvantage of a single bathroom.

"We can work around it," we told her.

Looking back, I see that the involuntary spasm that wracked Patti's body should have given us pause. But time was of the essence, and we REALLY liked everything else about the house, so we gave her a deposit on the spot.

Patti praised us for our "flexibility" as she popped a few nitroglycerin pills under her tongue and swallowed hard.

"Well," she said, "I guess that you know best what will work for you. How old did you say your children are?"

"Ten and twelve," Dale replied. "Why?"

"Just hold on to my card for the day you are ready to move up," Patti said. "It may be sooner than you think."

She burned rubber out of the driveway as she left to deposit the check.

But the single bathroom really wasn't that big of a deal. It took a little planning as far as getting ready for school and work, but frankly, Dale and I gloated for an entire year about what a GREAT deal we got. We continued to exult in our shrewd purchase until the fateful day Mark was struck by twin tragedies—testosterone and acne.

He would disappear into the bathroom for *hours* as he applied every facial cleansing product on the market ONE SKIN CELL AT A TIME while the rest of the family rioted in the hall or made up excuses to visit the neighbor's house.

Johnson & Johnson made a KILLING in the stock market that year.

So here we were three years later, standing in the hall with a screwdriver as we attempted to remove the bathroom door from its hinges. But, alas, I was the only thing that came unhinged that day.

"OUT!" I shrieked, hopping madly up and down like some kind of outlandishly awkward WASP break dancer.

"I just have to rinse off and I'll be right out," Mark called back from the shower, which had been continuously flowing for more than two hours.

"GET OUT NOW OR *I'LL* HAVE TO BE RINSED OFF!" I roared, to no avail.

"We need another bathroom," Dale insisted as we

waddled outside to the car so we could speed to the nearest all-night gas station to use a rest room, which, as it turned out, had apparently received its most recent cleaning during the coronation of Queen Elizabeth.

Mark was STILL in the shower when we returned home.

"We'll need about twenty thousand dollars for the remodeling job," I told Dale. "I already checked with a contractor last week. Even if they just turn the office into a bathroom, it is really expensive. But I really don't want to give up my office."

"You won't have to," she said. "We'll just make the office a combination bath and bedroom for Mark. He can sleep in the tub. It will make it so much more convenient for him, and you can have his old room for your office."

We got home and Dale went to the office and grabbed a calculator.

"Almost done," Mark called from the bathroom as the shower continued to flow.

Dale glared toward the hall and began pressing buttons.

"He is fifteen now. We legally have to provide him with shelter until he is eighteen. I will NOT endure this for three more years. So $20,000 divided by three years divided by 365 days in a year is . . . $18.26 per day for another bathroom," she said. "That's CHEAP compared to putting him in a hotel until he reaches voting age."

"Maybe it would just be simpler to look for a house with two bathrooms," I sighed.

"Almost done . . ." Mark called again from the bathroom.

We soon learned that "almost done" is a completely elastic and virtually meaningless phrase, in the same category as "Mideast peace process" (although it is conceivable that we will achieve an Arab-Israeli peace LONG before Mark learns to take a thirty-minute shower).

Mark finally emerged in a cloud of steam.

"Dale, look!" I cried. "It's the Creature From the Exceptionally Sanitary Lagoon!"

"Congratulations on single-handedly exhausting the municipal water system," Dale added. "I would ground you, but I can't risk having you within 100 feet of the bathroom all day long."

"Why don't you go hang out over at the house of someone we don't like very much?" I said.

Mark just shrugged.

"How come all the other kids got normal parents?" he muttered as he walked to his room.

"Two bathrooms," Dale said, staring at me with the desperate expression you typically only see on the face of a war refugee. "Tomorrow."

The following afternoon I picked up the phone and was just about to dial Patti's number when Brad charged in from school and rushed to the bathroom.

"I'm getting ZITS!" he gasped, staring into the vanity mirror. "Shelly said I'm getting big ZITS! I have to take a shower right now!"

The sharp click of the bathroom door being locked was disturbingly reminiscent of the sound in a scene from an old gangster movie wherein the warden locks away "Louie the Blade" for twenty years.

Dale and I exchanged a grim glance.

"He turned thirteen last week," she whispered.

"Testosterone," I muttered.

"Acne," she observed.

"We're doomed," I ventured.

"*Three* bathrooms," she said.

Before I took out a loan equal to the gross domestic product of Jamaica, I decided to find out how in the world families of the '40s and '50s, which were typically much larger than families today, used to make it with just one bathroom. We asked around.

Dale's mom, a registered nurse, found a plausible answer in a decades-old "family health" textbook.

"'For reasons of good hygiene, it is important to bathe at least once per week, with periodic sponge bathing as necessary on other days,'" she read aloud one evening as we all had dinner together.

"A bath once a week?!?" exclaimed Mark.

No wonder they could get by with only one bathroom—no one ever used it!

"And almost no one had two cars, either," Dale's mom added.

"Then what did the parents use?" Mark asked.

"The *parents* used the car, and the *kids* walked or rode bicycles or begged a ride from their parents," she replied.

"Barbarians!" Mark whispered before he fainted.

So Dale and I went back to the drawing board.

"So it wasn't just scheduling," I said later to Dale. "They literally didn't use the bath or shower as much as we do today."

After crunching the numbers every way we could, Dale and I came to the sober conclusion that we simply could not afford to either remodel *or* buy a new home unless I took on a second job, such as robbing convenience stores. While this can be lucrative, the last time we checked it was still forbidden by one of the Ten Commandments (even in the paraphrased versions—I looked it up).

So we decided on a more economical plan consisting of posting a "bathroom usage schedule" with escalating sanctions for each five minutes of overuse: beginning with a one-dollar fine, then working up to loss of video game privileges and ultimately ending with a prison sentence.

The very first day of the new program, Mark violated every time increment and earned every available sanction.

"There's a five-dollar bill on my dresser," he called from behind the shower as steam rolled from beneath the door.

"He is rapidly working himself into the running for being whacked with an economy-sized bottle of acne cleanser," Dale snapped.

"It's a good thing for him that isn't on the sanctions list," I chuckled.

"I added it," she said with no trace of mirth in her voice.

Because I am a perceptive and proactive husband, I sensed that this would be a very good time to take Dale out for coffee and safely away from large, blunt containers of facial care products.

We sat in a corner booth in the Downtown Espresso shop and sipped at double lattes.

"I'm just so frustrated that I don't know what to do," Dale said.

Her head dropped and I braced myself for the tears. But after a few tense moments, she began laughing.

I wasn't sure if this was a good or bad sign.

"Dale?" I said gently.

"Smelly natives," she said. "This is like the smelly natives."

"Um, let's go see the doctor," I advised as she laughed again.

"Do you remember that missionary we heard, gosh, fifteen years ago? The one who talked about the phases he went through when he moved to another culture?" she asked.

"Yes. Why?" I asked, completely lost.

"He said it started out by being fascinating, then it became frustrating, then funny, then fruitful."

"And this has something to do with never being able to use our bathroom?" I asked, truly puzzled.

Dale continued. "He said at first the experience was fascinating—being in a completely new culture and doing a completely different kind of work. Then he said it was frustrating, because he was surrounded by smelly people who were never on time and seemed to never change. It really started to bother him. Then he just learned to laugh. It was laugh or give up or go crazy. He just had to accept certain realities—it was laugh or cry. It was at that point that his ministry began to be fruitful. He stopped being mad at the smelly natives. He lightened up. And he started to see results. The kind of results that really mattered. Changes in the heart, even though, really, nothing else changed. He is still surrounded by smelly natives, but it is OK."

I frowned. "So you are saying . . . what? That we ship Mark off to some smelly land?"

Dale sighed. Then laughed again. "No. I am saying that we are in the same boat. These phases keep happening again and again, and it doesn't matter whether you are talking about missionary work or parenting. We are in a phase right now.

"Parenthood starts out to be fascinating—wow, we are going to have a baby! And then it quickly gets frustrating as the reality sets in—late-night feedings, exhaustion, messes, colic.

"But you eventually have to laugh, even at the frustrating things. Like when Mark was a toddler and learned to climb out of his crib. He used to wake up before our alarm went off, and then run to the refrigerator and you would bolt out of bed to catch him before he started dropping raw eggs on the floor."

"That was *so* bizarre," I mused. "What in the world made him do that? It drove me NUTS! Especially when he aimed for the CARPET."

But the mere memory made me start to snicker.

"Who *knows* what he was thinking?" Dale said, laughing hard. "It made us so uptight back then, but it is just funny now."

We both started to cackle at the memory.

"And look at us now," Dale said, wiping away a tear of mirth. "Look at what is driving us up the wall. He spends too much time in the bathroom. Yes, it is irritating, but it is a lot better than cleaning up raw eggs. And look at what we *aren't* fighting with him about. He isn't hanging out with a bad crowd, or flunking out of school, or stealing, or doing drugs, or any of a number of things a lot of families are struggling with. He carries a Bible to youth group—of his own free will! He has an internal moral compass. We have it so good as a family. We play together. We joke around. We are just *not* having serious problems right now. We need to be thankful."

"I would be more thankful if I didn't have to drive to Lenny's Jiffy Service to use the Jurassic toilet," I groused.

"I don't mean just ignore this problem," Dale said. "But let's stop coming so unglued. We are actually in a very fruitful phase of our life as parents and we shouldn't miss seeing it just because of the bathroom crisis."

Ultimately, we developed a fairly workable plan wherein Mark would make sure that all of us got to use the bathroom before he locked himself inside for three hours. We also strictly enforced a rule that stipulated Mark cannot shower on a Sunday morning— he MUST take care of that Saturday night—unless there are extraordinary extenuating circumstances, such as the rest of the family is vacationing in Brazil without him.

Over time, I actually perceived Mark becoming a little more disciplined and mature about use of the bathroom. In fact, I came in late one night from a business trip out of town and discovered that Mark was actually exiting the bathroom at 8:00 P.M.—a full ninety minutes earlier than what I had come to expect.

"Wow," I said to Dale. "He's ahead of schedule. I may be a theological conservative, but even I can recognize a sign from God when I see it."

Dale touched my hand gently and whispered,

"Actually, he got very behind. He just finished up yesterday's shower."

Then it was MY turn to starting throwing eggs.

I know some smelly natives who are going to have a new roommate REAL soon.

Chapter 21

The Shirt Off My Back (and the Socks Off My Feet)

When I was a little kid, some incredibly bright marketing guy came up with a bath product called Mr. Bubble. It was essentially just dishwashing liquid, only it was colored pink, scented like bubble gum, repackaged for kids, and sold at an enormous markup. But desperate mothers lunged at any product that implicitly promised their children would voluntarily adopt civilized standards of hygiene. So pink liquid soap became a big hit.

I REALLY liked this product.

For many years my favorite clothing article in the world was my Mr. Bubble T-shirt. I had clipped a valuable mail-in coupon from the back of a bottle of Mr. Bubble foaming bath liquid, sent in my hard-earned few dollars, and after a couple of weeks that seemed like FOREVER, I received the coolest shirt in the universe.

The shirt featured the pink, smiling face of Mr. Bubble on the front, and on the back, in big blue letters, was the message: "Makes getting clean twice as much fun as getting dirty!"

No one else in the neighborhood had a shirt like this, and I wore it with pride at every opportunity.

"No way!" Mark declared one day as I slipped "Mr. Bubble" over my head. "You are NOT wearing that to the lake. No other dad dresses like you do."

"Can't you act your age?" cried Brad.

Petty jealousy is so unbecoming to children. The shirt had arrived three weeks earlier and they were still clearly consumed with envy.

Regrettably, even Dale was exhibiting a distinctly unsanctified attitude about my new apparel.

"I will not be caught *dead* in public with you while you are wearing that ridiculous shirt," she said one day as we were getting ready to go shopping. "Why didn't you buy it when you were ten if you wanted one so badly?"

"I couldn't afford it when I was ten," I replied, hurt.

But I sensed that something deeper was lurking behind her sharp words.

"We can order one for you, too, if we can find another specially marked bottle that has a mail-in coupon," I said sympathetically.

She stared at me for a moment and replied, "I am really torn. I don't know if this comes under the section, 'For Better or for Worse' or 'In Sickness and in Health.'"

Mr. Bubble continued to be a source of contention with Dale and the kids. They all pretended to HATE Mr. Bubble, but they couldn't fool me. I recognize the grasping hand of covetousness when I see it.

As the spiritual leader of our home, I tried to assist them by reading relevant Scripture passages about envy at the dinner table, but they were in denial.

"WE HATE MR. BUBBLE, AND YOU LOOK LIKE A DORK!" they would shout in unison, almost as though they had been practicing this response together.

I chose to retire "Mr. Bubble" to my bottom drawer once they resorted to throwing household objects at me.

Then one day, a few years later, a new fad hit Brad's school. All the kids started showing up in "product" T-shirts. There were shirts advertising Campbell's Soup, the Pillsbury Dough Boy, candy bars, you name it.

Brad hunted through my dresser until he located "Mr. Bubble" and eagerly wore it to school the next day. No one else had one, and everybody wanted it.

"I thought you said it was humiliating," I said.

"Only when you wear it," he replied. "And where is your Spam shirt? I need that one too."

He ended up swiping all my coolest T-shirts.

I tried to fight for possession of these cherished garments, but Dale pointed out that Jesus said that if someone asks for your shirt, you should give him your cloak as well.

While the text didn't specifically mention the special commemorative Fiftieth Anniversary Spam shirt, I knew that she had me on the principle of the passage.

(NOTE TO MALE READERS: The moral of this episode is that you need to enjoy your childhood before you have children of your own, because otherwise you will suffer the little children swiping all your cool T-shirts.)

I no longer have any clothes I can call my own. (At least, not the kind that anyone actually sees when I am in public.)

What Mark and Brad have not nabbed for their own, Dale has laid claim to. She wears my down jacket when it is cold outside because she says that her coat is too thin. I offered to buy her one EXACTLY like mine, but she looked at me like I was a moron and replied, "Do you think I want to own a *man's* jacket?"

"Well, you wear mine all the time, so what's the difference?" I asked.

"I'm just borrowing yours," she said.

This line of reasoning is apparently perfectly rational to women, because all the guys I know complain about the way their wives steal clothes. But guys do not retaliate in like fashion. Guys do not swipe their wife's sweater when they feel a draft. Guys go to the closet to get their OWN sweat shirt (which isn't there because their wife swiped it already).

Between Dale and the kids, I have lost two coats, most of my socks, half of my sweat shirts, and virtually all my cool "tees" (including my prized "Spamburger" shirt).

This is not because I deprive my family of clothing. In fact, I have stuffed wads of cash in Dale's hands and virtually ordered her to go buy clothes. But she can't decide.

"Nothing looked good on me, and I refuse to waste money on something that I don't really like," she will say after a six-hour shopping spree that netted some replacement shoelaces.

But she will POUNCE on virtually anything casual I buy, no matter how ill fitting, because it is "comfortable."

So my only relief comes from buying clothes that are so dorky and uncomfortable that they are not remotely tempting to either Dale or the kids.

That's why I go to work every day in a starched white shirt, a tie, slacks, and burgundy wing-tip shoes. This isn't about fashion. It is the only thing left in my closet after the human locusts have descended.

If John the Baptist had a wife and kids, it goes a LONG way toward explaining why he wore a garment made of camel hair.

Chapter 22

Searching for the Good Old Days

All parents long for the "good old days" when it was easier to raise children because life moved at a more leisurely pace, kids were more respectful of authority, and if you escaped the plague you might live to be thirty-seven.

It doesn't matter in what age parents actually live—whether a thousand years ago or today—they all lament the period in history wherein it falls to them to raise children. And they sigh wistfully for that "better day" when it would have been easier/safer/happier than it is in (fill in the year) to raise kids.

The refrain has basically been the same over time: Things were better back when . . .

1. most people lived on a farm, or
2. Eisenhower was president, or
3. the Mongol horde only burned half the village.

(Historians have unearthed evidence that parents who lived several centuries ago were making many of the same comments as parents today, with the exception that "Turn that stereo DOWN!" used to be "Turn that flute and harp DOWN!")

Generally speaking, parental concerns of 99 B.C. are the same concerns parents are expressing in 1999. We all want our kids to grow up safe and happy and become well-adjusted and successful adults, and we wish the task were easier than it is today.

But I am not sure that any age really has a legitimate claim to the designation of "the worst of times" for parenting (with the possible exception of the 1970s, when the entire industrialized world was afflicted with a mass outbreak of disco music).

Nor am I convinced that there has ever been a "golden age" of parenting. I don't think that earlier times were necessarily simpler, unless your definition of "simple" includes eking out a living by hunting down and eating random animals, or fighting off periodic raids by a neighboring clan, or contracting scurvy on a three-month ocean voyage, or living in a cramped apartment with three other families and working twelve hours per day, or losing one or two children to untreatable childhood diseases.

Even if you jump forward to fairly recent American history, parents have experienced the hardships imposed by wars (both a civil war and several foreign conflicts, including two world wars), economic calamity (the Great Depression stands out), and the periodic ravages of nature (hurricanes, tornadoes, floods, droughts, and Elvis impersonators).

I am grateful to be raising my sons in an era of relative peace and prosperity, enormous advances in medicine and technology, and a high likelihood that I will live to see my grandchildren and even great-grandchildren. Having said that, however, I also think that the late twentieth century may, in fact, have a credible claim on being one of the darker times in which to raise children—at least in American history.

At the risk of seeming to idealize that mythical "golden age" I have just pooh-poohed, the fact remains that there was a time, attested to by LOTS of older folks, when society was, in fact, a more civil, kind, and safe place to be.

Even in neighborhoods and communities that were dirt poor by today's standards, my parents and grandparents have spoken of unlocked doors, low crime, and children playing unsupervised and yet safely in the ball field down at the school in the waning daylight. They speak of communities turning out to build the barn a farmer lost to a fire, of orphaned children being "taken in" and raised by a neighbor family, of generosity amid poverty far deeper than most of us can imagine enduring.

While crime and selfishness and hate have existed since Cain murdered his brother, Abel, there is something deeper and darker and, well, worse about society today. It is increasingly common to read a newspaper account of kids murdering other kids on the school grounds. And we hear bewildering reports of teens randomly spraying bullets from a car just for the excitement of killing unknown victims. And there are "artists" who make millions of dollars by selling music that focuses on killing police officers and savagely abusing women.

This is a downward lurch into depravity at a magnitude unheard of before. This level of evil did not exist when my parents were children, when sneaking a package of gum into class was risky business. There are schools today that are virtually open marketplaces for drugs and weapons and where teachers live in mortal fear of assault by students.

My own two boys tell me about some VERY spooky kids on campus who choose to dress entirely in black and who are known as "Mansons"—disciples of a most foul and profane young musician who glories in despising all that is holy or good, all in the name of "entertainment."

I have seen these kids. And they are not kids. They are human ghouls, who wear spiked collars and who dress in chains and shirts with bizarre messages like "Be your own God." They are lost souls who delight in advertising their lostness.

There was nothing even remotely like this when I was a kid.

I visited recently with my fifth grade teacher, Mrs. Dinnean, who had just celebrated her ninetieth birthday. Her eyes danced as I came into the room.

In the course of our conversation, she shook her head and noted that "teaching is much more difficult today—the discipline problem."

Translation: In her day—in MY day, for that matter—children behaved in class and feared being sent to the principal's office because he would paddle you a good one if you mouthed off to a teacher—and then your dad would paddle you again when you got home.

That was pretty much the norm from the earliest days of public education in this nation until around the 1960s, when the nation started going to hell in a big way. I use that term in a theological sense. Something extremely weird happened about thirty years ago, when a big segment of society rejected the noble and the good to embrace the ignoble and the base.

And the stupid.

All kinds of really idiotic and damaging theories went mainstream back then, such as: hallucinogenic chemicals will enlighten you, and there is something very free about having sex with lots of different people, and you can't trust anyone over thirty unless he is Dr. Timothy Leary (and you are doing drugs with him), and anything that infringes on your selfishness is bad and should be rejected.

And out of that nonsense emerged a subculture of people who often ingest lots of chemicals and have lots of random sex that produces lots of random babies who grow up into disconnected teenagers who dress in black and spray lots of random bullets and don't even realize they have done anything wrong, because they seriously do not understand the concept of right and wrong.

And I sigh wistfully for a time that I can still touch as I hold the hand of a ninety-year-old retired teacher and wish that my boys could be in her class, far from the gangs and drugs and teenage sex in an age that was poorer and harder and much, much better.

But Mrs. Dinnean is growing tired, and it is time for me to step outside and back into my own time.

And mine is the age of the Mansons.

The chains.

The ghouls.

And I have no choice in the matter.

And neither did believing parents during the darkest days of the Roman Empire.

And neither did faithful moms and dads who held

their children close as Adolf Hitler raged and shrapnel fell like hail in a storm.

So like generations of Christian parents before me, I bow my head and pray for my family.

For my boys.

And for the lost ones.

Chapter 23

Boys Will Be Boys (Like, Duh, What Else Would They Be?)

There are subtle but significant differences between little girls and little boys, much like there are subtle but significant differences between a daisy and a bazooka.

As a parent or prospective parent of boys, you need to be aware of these contrasts. If you are going to base your parental expectations strictly on your observations of the nice little family down the block where the children consist exclusively of little girls, you are in for one way-big rude awakening.

Please consult my handy, patented "gender differences chart for children" to get a sense of what I mean.

Little Girls	Little Boys
1. Hug	1. Hit
2. Giggle	2. Fight
3. Hold hands	3. Make bodily noises

These differences have NOTHING to do with the environment in which children are raised, and if you have boys, then you need to accept the fact that

NOTHING you can do will change the fact that deeply imbedded in their DNA, right next to the hair color gene, is:

1. the "get dirty" gene
2. the "pick your nose" gene, and
3. the "hey, let's set off some fireworks!" gene.

You can no more change these hereditary traits than you can turn a cheetah into a tofu-consuming, vegetarian zealot. Nevertheless, there are shrill, ideologically driven crusaders who for decades have tried to convince parents that if only we would cast aside our stereotypes and focus on raising boys and girls identically, the end result would be a nation of healthy, balanced young people who would equally participate in all career paths—including the defensive line for the 49ers—and differ only in who has to wear a bra.

Yeah, right.

This premise ignores truckloads of empirical data that clearly indicate that throughout the centuries and across all racial and geographic boundaries, little girls have been hugging and giggling and holding hands, while boys have been hitting, fighting, and producing various bodily noises (pausing only when they got some fireworks).

I can attest from personal experience that the genetic male impulse to ignite fireworks is so powerful that it is completely uncontrollable. This is probably why the Bible does not forbid it, any more than it forbids breathing.

I first experienced the potent effect of the fireworks gene when I was seven years old. My brothers and I collected soda bottles for weeks and exchanged them at Frankie's Market for enough loot to buy a small arsenal of fireworks. We then scampered home to await evening so we could set them off.

Regrettably, in the state in which we lived at that time, evening did not fall at two o'clock in the afternoon. So we began to get restless and twitchy. We waited and waited and finally tried setting off a sparkling fountain at 2:04 P.M. but the sun was still far too bright and the result was anemic and unsatisfying. We tried moving into shade, but that was not much better.

It finally occurred to one of us that it was VERY dark inside the tool shed. The fact that the shed was made of wood, and was roughly eight feet long and four feet wide, and that, when you included the neighbor boys, five of us would need to crowd into it, did not immediately strike any of us as a serious obstacle. Such is the influence of the fireworks gene.

After we extinguished the flames, we decided that there was a flaw in our approach. So we put the spark-emitting fireworks away and shifted to smoke bombs. This quickly escalated into a game of "dare" in which we would all get in the shed, set off a smoke bomb, and dare each other to stay in the shed until everyone else had bailed out to gag and retch on the lawn. This was every bit as fun and stupid and dangerous as it sounds. It is a wonder we were not asphyxiated, especially when we elevated the contest to the point that we were locking each other in the shed.

Needless to say, no little girls participated in this event, occupied as they were with hugging and giggling and holding hands.

Years later, I was not at all surprised when my own

young boys fell under the strong influence of the fireworks gene.

We were on a family trip, driving from northern California to Memphis, Tennessee, during June of 1995. It was on that trip we discovered that New Mexico basically consists of a string of Dairy Queens, gas stations, and fireworks stands that sell stuff we could NO WAY ever buy in California, including surface-to-air missiles.

Mark and Brad and I bought tons of these explosive devices and set them off whenever we got bored along the highway, which was about every six minutes.

Dale was not enjoying it nearly as much as the male faction of our family. In fact, she was so unamused that she even resisted the female impulse to hug us and giggle and hold our hands.

"Why don't we try to reach Memphis before we reach senility?" she would ask as we launched another round of bottle rockets.

We finally reached our destination, where we were able to take in many interesting sights, such as the Mississippi River at night during a fireworks show, and a Methodist Church parking lot on the outskirts of town, where we basically replicated a scale model of a World War II bombing run on Berlin.

Dale finally dragged us off to a bunch of museums and art galleries and historic sites and just about anything else she could find that didn't involve matches.

You may recall from the book of Genesis that, following each of His creative works, God saw that "it was good"—until He created Adam. It was at that point that He said, "It is NOT good for the man to be alone."

Bible scholars will tell you that the Lord's statement about Adam was extremely emphatic. God was saying, in very strong terms, "It is NOT GOOD AT ALL for the man to be alone! No way! This is ABSOLUTELY unacceptable!"

He then knocked Adam completely unconscious and rapidly created Eve. You will notice that God did not give Adam the capacity to reproduce by cellular division. There is a good reason for this. An exclusively male world would have been completely torched within a week without the moderating effect of women.

No, God wisely created men and women as different but complementary genders who can complete each other, meet each other's physical and emotional needs, nurture a family, have fun, and also restrain each other's excesses.

I am personally very thankful for these differences for all of the aforementioned reasons, but also because my tool shed is still intact.

So the key point here is that you, as a parent of boys, need to accept the fact that your boys will act like boys, not girls, as they are growing up, and then when they are adults they will continue to act like boys, so the key to their future is to just try to keep them sort of under control until they move out, and take all the matches out of their suitcase when they are not looking, and pray that they meet a great young woman and settle down and then the whole mess is off your hands and she gets to deal with it and you have no more legal liability.

And then when you have grandchildren, if any of them are boys, do NOT let them near your tool shed.

Chapter 24

The Final Word

Writing a book is a lot like giving birth, only there is more yelling involved and you don't get to bill the insurance company at the end.

For me, it isn't the writing part that is hard. It is the not-writing part that is so difficult.

I could crank out a whole herd of books were it not for the fact that, in between writing, I have to work at my day job, actually try to parent my boys, repair domestic appliances, eat, sleep, tell Mark to leave Brad alone, carve out quality time with Dale, take the dog to "Jennifer's Clip and Shave Palace," teach a Sunday school class, tell Brad to leave Mark alone, get the car repaired, pay bills, dump chemicals into the pool, tell Mark and Brad to leave each other alone THIS INSTANT or they are both grounded, get the tires rotated, clean the garage, get the flu, entertain guests for dinner (long after the flu part), buy stamps, tell Mark and Brad to leave Mom alone, attend a school band concert, remember our anniversary, pay the taxes, and you get the general idea.

I started writing about my family when Mark was just a baby, so the book you are holding is the equivalent of a sixteen-year pregnancy. Kind of makes you shudder, doesn't it, ladies?

But the total time I actually spent writing during all those years was probably just a couple of months.

Writing is a breeze.

Life is the hard part.

Some authors will whine and complain about how challenging and laborious and difficult it is to write. Well, sure it is if you are Leo Tolstoy or Ernest Hemingway. But not for me.

As I told Mark and Brad one day, "Just think. I am getting paid to make fun of you! This is a parent's dream come true!"

While I was wrestled to the ground and tickled unmercifully for making that statement, it is nevertheless true. This is WAY more fun than mowing the lawn or doing laundry or banging out a report at work or doing any of a number of other possible activities. So I have no sympathy for other authors, especially the ones who write serious stuff. If John Calvin had spent his time poking fun at his kids instead of creating a systematic theology, he would have been a much more chipper guy (even though the church would be stupider as a result).

So I guess we do need serious authors as well, but I don't have to be one of them in order to make a significant contribution to the world. If you have laughed along with me, if you have smiled at situations in your own family that used to drive you nuts, if you are less uptight as a parent because you realize you are not alone and that ALL boys are this way, if you found anything I said to be useful, then I have succeeded.

Additionally, you may be interested to discover that the publishing firm that bought my manuscript and created this book is actually a ministry organization. A percentage of the profits generated by this book will help fund missionaries and a Christian college. It's true!

So not only do I get paid for poking fun at my kids, but I get to help fulfill the Great Commission at the same time. Somebody pinch me. Is this a great country or what?

"So what in the world is your point and where are you going with this train of thought?" you may be asking yourself.

I have no idea.

Boys will do that to you. You start out as a bright, energetic, thoughtful individual and then you become a parent and you can barely complete a coherent sentence unless it is something short and to the point like "No!"

So where were we?

Oh, yeah. I started out by saying that producing this book has taken WAY too long. But I have finally reached the last chapter, and I have to give it a profound and poignant ending to tie everything together.

So I will leave you with this short anecdote that really captures the core essence of your male child. This powerful story could give you a keen insight into the heart and soul of your boy.

Back when Dale and I were teaching fifth grade Sunday school, we typically brought a snack—such as donuts or Oreos or, in a pinch, little packets of restaurant sugar—for our class.

Word got around to the high school students that

we usually had extra goodies left over, so we began to get mobbed at the end of each class by a group of rowdy boys who displayed all the manners and finesse you would expect from a swarm of beggars on the streets of ancient Jericho during a famine.

The weekly raid was getting expensive, so Dale and I devised a brilliant strategy to dispense with them.

Any professional sociologist who deals with teen males will tell you that young men are OBSESSED with their image and how they are viewed by their peer group. This is a well-documented aspect of teen behavior. So, armed with this knowledge, Dale and I imposed a condition one Sunday morning as the rabble began to gather at the door to our Sunday school class.

"OK," I said, addressing the first of the throng. "You can have an Oreo on the condition that you drop down on one knee and declare in a loud voice, 'Dave and Dale are wonderful and special people who are my superiors in every way.'"

The horde was suddenly silent.

The leader of the pack, who dresses way cool all the time and has each hair carefully put into place each morning by a team of professional cosmeticians, stared at us for a moment and we could literally read his mind.

These people are asking me to abjectly humiliate myself in front of all my friends for a single cookie that I can go buy for myself right after church.

He took a deep breath.

"If I say it twice, do I get two Oreos?" he asked, dropping to one knee and loudly proclaiming how wonderful and special Dale and I were, and freely confessing that we were his superiors in every way.

The rest of the herd followed suit, so Dale nervously flung cookies at the advancing assemblage as they lined up to pay us homage.

The Bible records that Esau sold his birthright for a bowl of soup.

A few thousand years later, an entire class of high school boys publicly abased themselves for an Oreo.

There is a powerful moral lesson in this story, but I don't think you want to know what it is.